POINT, CLICK, **QUILT!**

Turn Your Photos into Fabulous Fabric Art

16 Projects • Fusible Appliqué, Thread Sketching & More

Susan Brubaker Knapp

C&T PUBLISHING

Publisher: Amy Marson

Creative Director: Gailen Runge

Acquisitions Editor: Susanne Woods

Editor: Liz Aneloski

Technical Editor: Nanette S. Zeller

Copyeditor/Proofreader: Wordfirm Inc.

Cover Designer: Kristen Yenche

Book Designer: Christina D. Jarumay

Production Coordinator: Zinnia Heinzmann

Production Editor: Julia Cianci

Illustrator: Tim Manibusan

Quilt Photography by Christina Carty-Francis and Diane Pedersen of C&T Publishing, Inc., and how-to and inspirational photography by Susan Brubaker Knapp, unless otherwise noted

Published by C&T Publishing, Inc., P.O. Box 1456, Lafayette, CA 94549

Library of Congress Cataloging-in-Publication Data

Knapp, Susan Brubaker.

Point, click, quilt! : turn your photos into fabulous fabric art 16 projects : fusible appliqué, thread sketching & more / Susan Brubaker Knapp.

    p. cm.

ISBN 978-1-60705-226-5 (softcover)

1. Quilting--Patterns. 2. Transfer-printing. 3. Drawing from photographs. I. Title.

TT835.K563 2011

746.46--dc22

2010046183

Printed in China

10 9 8 7 6 5 4 3 2 1

DEDICATION

To my daughters, Lea and Julia, who are always teaching me how to see—and to my mother, Eleanor Carter Brubaker (1936–2011)

ACKNOWLEDGMENTS

Many thanks to…

my supportive husband, Rob,

the entire creative team at C&T Publishing,

and my friends in the Pandoras, Fiber Art Options, and Lake Norman Quilters.

37   40   43   46

CONTENTS

63   67   73   78

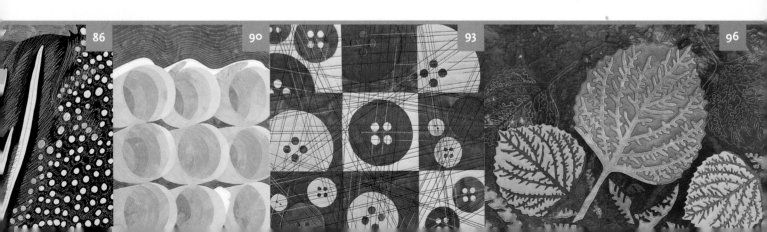

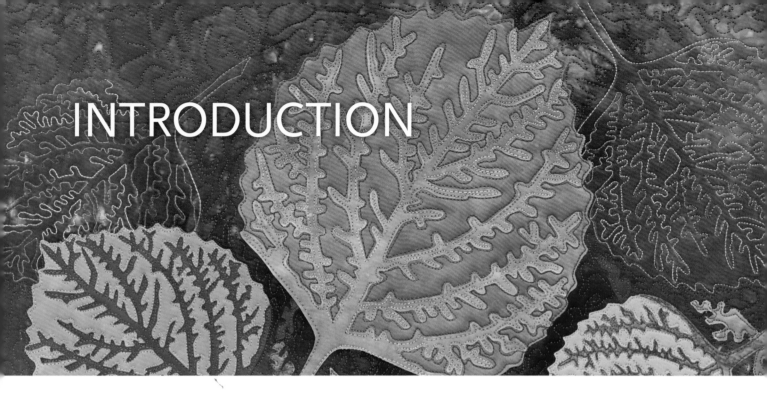

INTRODUCTION

While I have always enjoyed taking photos, it took me a while to realize how much photography could be a part of my artistic process. Like much of what I do now for a living, I have never studied it in a classroom. My brother and parents shared a darkroom space in our back basement when I was a teenager, but I completely ignored it. My first real desire to take better photos began about a decade ago when I had my first child and wanted to take shots to capture the wonder of those first amazing days.

Several years ago, I started taking photographs in a more deliberate way. I began thinking about photography almost as a form of meditation or deep study of what was. When you take photography seriously, it forces you to be in the moment, and an hour or two spent shooting in a garden, on a city street, or on a mountain hike can leave you serene and perfectly centered, and at the same time bursting with creative energy.

Perhaps you already enjoy taking photos, or have at least taken snapshots of vacations or special occasions. If so, this book is a guide to thinking about photography in a different way, as a way of truly learning to see and appreciate what is around you and to record it in a meaningful way. The kinds of subjects you find most interesting will teach you much about what you enjoy, what attracts you, and what you want to communicate through your work. And the shots you take will provide you with a deep well of ideas and images you can use.

The first chapters of this book include concrete information about how to take better photos, based on the elements of art and basic design principles. They include specific suggestions and tips and a series of "missions" you can do on your own or with friends that will start you down the path of learning to see with an artist's eye. You don't need a lot of materials or equipment, just an inexpensive digital camera and the desire to try looking at the world in a different way.

This book does not include projects that deal with the human face or form, which are the subject of other excellent books specifically on the subject. The projects here, based on my photos, are a great way to learn new techniques. Some are realistic subjects, some explore the process of abstraction, and some use materials that may be new to you. Try a few of my projects and then go out and take photos for projects you can make completely your own.

Susan

CREATIVITY AND LEARNING TO SEE

Creativity involves not only imagining great new things, but acting on that imagining. It is a process of considering new possibilities, combinations, connections, or alternatives and then using those ideas to solve a problem or to communicate an idea or value. For the visual artist, creativity begins with what I call "learning to see."

The difference between looking and seeing is akin to the difference between existing and living. Looking is passive, but when you see, you form an intimate connection with what you are viewing.

Here's an example. You are walking down a sidewalk in your neighborhood, past a neighbor's hydrangea bush in bloom. "That's pretty," you think, and keep walking.

You have just looked at the hydrangea, but you have not really seen it. Go back. Notice the way the recent rain has left raindrops on the petals that reflect sparkles of blue sky; the way the new growth is a marvelous chartreuse green next to the duller green older growth; the perfect symmetry of the leaves; the vein structure and the tightly curled buds with tiny sections, waiting to open; the first blush of lavender blue on the pale green-white flowers; the marvelous serrated edge of the leaves lined in a lighter green.

How has this experience of seeing made you more creative? You have opened your eyes—and perhaps your mind and soul—to the amazing things around you. You have perceived structure and line, color and texture.

Now, ask yourself, "What if…?" and "Could I…?" What if I created a piece in just ten shades of green? What if I created a flower three-dimensionally, using tiny tufts of organza? Could I drop color out of the equation entirely and concentrate on the line and shape of the leaves instead? Could I focus on the water drops, and what is reflected in them?

The mere act of slowing down, of taking the time to see the hydrangea, may make you more creative, because your brain has more time to form connections and consider possibilities. Photography, the act of composing and taking your shots, slows you down even more, giving you even more time to ponder those important "What if" and "Could I" questions.

And in taking the time to do this activity, you have declared that it is important to you, worthy of your attention. That alone will make you more creative.

How to Shoot Great Photos That Will Make Great Quilts

Here are some of the guiding principles that good photographers know, whether they've learned them intuitively or been taught them in a classroom. Start putting them to work, and you'll soon be shooting more dynamic photos.

1. **Shoot vertically as well as horizontally.** It is natural for people to shoot horizontally, since that is the way we see the world, through two eyes arrayed horizontally, our peripheral vision filling in on the far left and right. But some subjects beg to be shot in a vertical format. Just turn your camera and try shooting your subject both ways.

2. **Be patient.** Don't be afraid to arrange your subjects or wait for them to get into just the right position. You may also have to wait for the light to be correct. If the subject is interesting but the light is wrong, come back at a different time of day, or even a different season.

This sheep pasture, normally a pleasant meadow, looks foreboding with the bare trees of autumn and an approaching storm.

3. **Change position so you have something interesting in the foreground.** It can be a person, a tree branch, or a flower. This adds to the perspective of the shot, creates a sense of depth, and often makes for a livelier photo.

Belly down in the sand, I took this photo, which speaks to the perfect vastness of the beach, with its billions of grains of sand. It would be unremarkable without the weathered shell in the foreground.

4. **Look at things from all angles.** Don't just shoot head on. Shoot very low and very high. Think about the way a crawling baby might perceive things versus a giraffe or a construction worker on a scaffold up 40 stories. Shoot straight down from the tops (or high windows) of tall buildings. Shoot up while lying flat on your back in the forest.

A high vantage point from a skyscraper looking down into a park gives an unusual perspective and throws a landscape into a fractured set of planes and textures.

5. **Watch for unpredictable details.** Small, unexpected things are what set great photos apart from average ones. They sometimes include subtle meanings or symbolism that can make a piece of art based on them more powerful.

The newly repaired spokes in the oxcart, not yet painted, speak to the craftsmanship and care of the cart owner, and of a time before our current throwaway culture.

The tiny birds perched in the spiny ocotillo offer a perfect natural counterpoint to the man-made bells and cross of the mission tower.

6. Use lines to move the eye across the composition. Remember that the characteristics and rotation of the line can change the tone of the photo and how dynamic it seems.

Horizontal lines like those in these ocean waves are static, calm, and predictable.

Vertical lines imply action. Diagonal lines give a feeling of movement. Curving diagonals add grace and elegance.

7. Salvage what you can. You don't always have time to compose the perfect shot. Remember that a section of your photo may be perfect for what you need, even if the whole isn't. You can also delete or add elements from different photos.

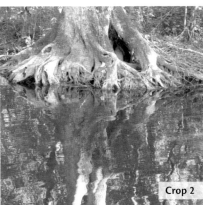

Crop 2

Original photo

Crop 1

Crop 3

When shooting this photo of tree roots along the edge of a swamp river (see original photo), I was in a boat that was quickly carrying me away from the subject. I didn't panic. I knew I could crop this into a great shot later. Here are three possibilities cropped from the same shot.

8. Shoot, shoot, shoot. While working as a journalist, I learned from newspaper photographers that the best way to get a great shot is to take a ton of photos. If you are lucky, you get one good shot in a hundred. With digital cameras, there's no film or processing charges, so there's really no excuse not to do this.

Sometimes it is not a matter of which photo is the best, but more a case of which photo appeals to you, or what you are trying to say with your art. When shooting these photos of two nearly identical structures painted different colors in Colonial Williamsburg, I was intrigued with their simplicity, and their graphic nature and clean lines. They are almost like Monopoly houses. When choosing a photo to use for an art quilt, I'd look for the one that most clearly showed these things.

Photo 1 shows the overall scene, and the white oyster-shell road leads the eye toward the red and white structures. Photo 2 has a nice patch of white oyster-shell road in the lower left corner, and the houses are slightly off center, which is nice. In Photo 3, the houses are right in the center of the composition, and the white road is gone. Photo 4 shows just the red house, and from a different angle, which makes the house silhouette less graphic than before. It also includes details, such as the light, that I think detract from what appealed to me about these houses. If I were choosing one photo to make into an art quilt, I'd probably choose the third one, but perhaps add in a patch of white road at the left corner.

9. **Pay attention to the rule of thirds.** A composition divided exactly in half looks too balanced, too static and predictable. Dividing the composition in thirds sets it slightly off balance, adding interest.

If you follow the rule of thirds, this often means that you will place your subject off center, which makes it more dynamic than if it were smack dab in the middle of your photo.

It is sometimes helpful to think of a tic-tac-toe board positioned over the image. Place your subject at one of the intersections, or use it to fill one-third or two-thirds of the frame.

These three photos demonstrate the rule of thirds. In the first, the ship takes up the right two-thirds of the shot. In the second, the main part of the castle takes up the bottom third, and the parapet takes up the middle third. Some of the focal points also fall at key intersections. The off-center barrel in the third shot would be far less interesting if it were positioned right in the middle of this shot.

10. **Consider negative space.** Negative space is the space around your main subject, where not much is happening in your photo, or where there are few details. In land-scapes, it is often the sky. Negative space is important, though. It provides breathing room around the subject, a resting spot for the eye. It often provides context, and can change the tone and weight of your piece.

I shot this photo because the oncoming storm had turned the sky a dark slate-blue color, and the filtered light made the trees a fascinating chartreuse color. The negative space around the tree foliage and lights adds drama to an ordinary scene.

11. **Pick odd numbers of things.**
When shooting a group of objects, three is usually better than two, five better than four.

The photo of three coneflowers is more interesting than the photo with two.

If your photo has an even number, consider deleting or adding one, as I did in this piece, "I Didn't Know Roses Had Hips."

Design and Composition Basics

A piece of art is thought to have unity or harmony—a state of wholeness or completion—when the elements and principles of art are used correctly. Elements of art include line, size, value, texture, shape, form, and color. In "On a Mission" (pages 17–28), I discuss these elements and provide exercises to help you learn to take photos that capture each. Unfortunately, there is no formula, magic potion, or list of ingredients that will make a piece of art successful, and no agreement on exactly what the list of design principles should include. Some of the best art breaks the rules.

Nevertheless, the following principles provide a helpful framework artists use to create and evaluate their work.

Focal Point or Center of Interest

Most art has a focal point. It is the place where your eye naturally rests, the center of attention, the primary subject. The focal point is easy to spot in art that has a single subject. In a piece of art with many objects or subjects in it, you can draw the viewer's eye to the focal point by using color, contrast, size, and movement. Art can have a primary focal point and one or more minor focal points.

Contrast/Variety

Including dissimilar elements increases interest and pulls attention to the focal point. These include the contrasts between light and dark, hard and soft, thick and thin, straight and curved, rough and smooth, large and small.

The darkness of the building and its shadow stands out in strong contrast to the brightly lit grass and wall.

The fuzzy organic shrub contrasts nicely with a man-made stone wall.

Balance

The concept of balance explores the relationship between opposing elements. There are many ways to achieve balance, which has more to do with creating a harmonious composition than with making things equal.

Symmetrical balance can be achieved by placing the subject right in the middle of the photo, or by placing two subjects of equal size or visual weight equidistant from the center, like two toddlers on a seesaw.

This photo of a door demonstrates symmetrical balance.

This shot of a sugar maple in autumn demonstrates radial balance, where the elements radiate outward from the center.

With asymmetrical balance, elements can be arranged unevenly, but work well together to achieve balance. In radial balance, the movement is out from the center.

While you don't want your work to be harshly unbalanced, a little something to throw it slightly off balance is welcome. In the photos illustrating different kinds of balance, note that the green plants to the left of the door pull your eye in that direction once you've examined the interesting shapes on the door. Similarly, in the tree shot, the massive trunk is more dominant on the left side of the frame.

Repetition

Repeating one or more of the elements of design (such as line or color) can create movement, rhythm, or pattern.

In this photo, the strong green vertical lines and orange wedges are repeated, creating pattern and a sense of rhythm.

Movement

Lines add movement by guiding the eye toward the major and minor focal points. Diagonal lines add the greatest sense of movement.

The sinuous lines of the railing lead the eye from the lower left toward the upper right.

The diagonal lines along the edges of the fountain and the arcing lines of water pull the viewer's eye toward the woman and child.

Figure and Ground

The background of a photo is its setting; in landscapes, this is most often the sky. Normally, the background is lighter than the subject; when this is reversed, it creates wonderful ambiguity.

Silhouetting figures draws attention to the stances of the people, as well as the beautiful blue background.

The view through an ornate window—a building in a Chinese garden—is more interesting because dark tones naturally recede, while light tones come forward. But in this case, the dark areas are in the foreground.

From Photo to Quilt

In creating a quilt based on a photo, it is important to remind yourself that you do not need to accurately re-create the photo. If the photo has flaws or does not meet some of the basic design principles, you can always change it when you make your art quilt.

Journalists draw a distinction between photographs and what they call "photo illustrations." In a photo, nothing is changed. The shutter snaps and records the image in front of the photographer's eyes, and that is that. But a photo illustration is a purposeful manipulation of the image to tell a story, set a mood, or create something that does not exist in reality.

When working from your photos to create art quilts, you can choose to faithfully reproduce your photo, or you can take the photo illustration approach. You can delete undesirable elements, add elements that make the piece stronger or tell the story better, replace backgrounds, change colors, slide the focal point to a different place, or any number of other things.

This purposeful cutting, pasting, merging, and manipulating is part of what makes an art quilt a piece of art.

Developing an Image Bank

Artists understand the importance of keeping a sketchbook. The process of making a sketchbook, and the discipline required to do so, helps you explore and store ideas, themes, possibilities, and ways of expressing yourself. As someone not formally trained as an artist, I have tried hard—and fairly unsuccessfully!—to maintain a sketchbook. But I do faithfully update what I call my "image bank." It serves many of the same purposes as a sketchbook.

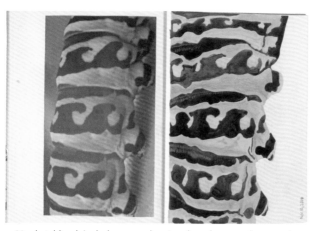

My sketchbook includes many drawings based on my photographs.

To create your own photo/image bank, the first step is to regularly take photos and to make a conscientious effort to improve your skills and explore new themes. After a photo shoot or a vacation to a new place, it is important to do four things:

Edit. First, go through all your shots and put them in three categories: pitches, maybes, and saves. The maybes are shots that have something you find interesting, even if the shot as a whole is not great.

Upload. Keep the saves and the maybes in an online photo account, such as Snapfish, Shutterfly, Kodak Gallery, Fotki, or SmugMug. Each company has somewhat different features. Many are free and offer you unlimited storage of your photos and an easy way to retrieve and download a full-resolution image whenever you need it again.

Back up. While an online photo account provides backup of your images, there's no guarantee that the service won't go out of business or have a problem that could compromise your files. So I recommend backing up your photos on a separate hard drive as well. And once every six months or so, copy all your photos onto a DVD and put it in your safe deposit box.

Print. Have prints made of the best shots, the ones you might want to use in the future, and put them in an album. I use archival-quality sleeves, and I categorize the images. Plants go in one place, animals, landscapes, and so on in another. This photo album is a source of images and inspiration whenever the creative well runs dry.

I keep my most interesting images in a photo album.

Copyright Issues

Simply put, it is illegal and unethical to use other people's photos or images without their permission. Under American copyright law, unless a photo or image is in the "public domain," you may not use it in your work unless you get permission from the artist. Photographers are sometimes willing to grant this permission, provided that they are given credit for the photograph whenever your quilt is displayed. Some will charge a fee to use it as the basis for your work.

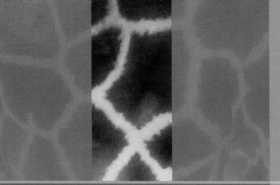

The missions and exercises in this section are designed to help you learn to shoot more creative photos that can be used to create great quilts. Along the way, practice the principles of composition covered in Design and Composition Basics (pages 12–15).

Try not to shoot photos for a specific project. If you are too focused on one particular project, it can limit what you allow yourself to see. If you are worrying about what you are going to do with a particular photo, you can't be open to new ideas that present themselves.

Don't be afraid. Just jump in. Allow yourself to play, to be spontaneous, to try new things. Granting yourself permission to play is essential to creativity. If you feel a bit hesitant to get started, enlist a friend—or better yet, a group of friends—to go on your mission with you. You'll feel braver, and your ideas and curiosity will rub off on each other.

So, as they used to say at the start of each episode of the 60s television show *Mission: Impossible*, "Your mission, should you decide to accept it …"

MISSION NO. 1:

Shoot for Line, Color, Shape/Form, Light/Shadow, Reflection, Texture/Pattern, or Angle

This is a good exercise to do over a week or two. Each day, go out of your house with your camera thinking, "I'm only going to take photos of _____ today." Fill in the blank from the list below, and you'll be amazed at what you find.

Line: Look for straight lines, curvy lines, and angular lines; parallel lines and lines that intersect; lines that seem orderly and neat, and lines that suggest chaos.

Color: Pick a color. Take a piece of paper and jot down as many words as you can think of that describe a color (for green, you might write down emerald, sage, sea-glass, lime, chartreuse, celadon, olive, kelly, pine). Then go out and shoot that color, in all its glorious permutations.

Shape/Form: Just shoot squares or rectangles, triangles or circles. Grab a friend or your child and make it into a scavenger hunt. See how many of each shape you can find in an hour. When you come home, look closely at all your photos. Which ones draw your eye, and why?

Light/Shadow: Choose a sunny day and find a time of day when shadows are long (generally between eight and ten in the morning and four and six in the afternoon). Go out and search for shadows. Note how they are distorted when they fall across objects, how colors change when they are in shadow.

Reflection: Go out in search of reflective surfaces like mirrors, windows, puddles, and calm water. Think about how the reflection is different from the reflected object.

Texture/Pattern: Both organic and synthetic materials can be rich in texture. Try to ignore the colors of what you are shooting and look for texture. Consider shooting in black-and-white mode, if your camera permits this.

Exercises

Trace and recolor. Print one of your photos at 8″ × 10″ or larger and place a piece of tracing paper over it. Use a fine-tip black pen to trace the dominant lines in the photo. Then, photocopy this traced drawing so you have a black-and-white line drawing. Use colored pencils or markers to color in the drawing using different colors from the original photo. How does this change the mood or feel of the original? Has it become more abstract?

What is the strongest feature?

Take a group of photos you have shot recently and sort it into piles, according to dominant feature—line, color, shape/form, light/shadow, reflection, texture/pattern, and angle. Count how many photos are in each pile. The number will tell you a lot about what interests you. Consider forcing yourself to shoot one of the categories that you usually neglect.

If you have many photos that fall into the texture category, for example, think about whether you are addressing this in your work. Color is seductive. Many people are so mesmerized by it that they ignore the other things that make photos strong. If you have a category with only a few photos, take photos that focus on that feature next time you shoot. Force yourself to work outside your comfort zone for a short time.

Just because a photo is strong in one area does not mean that it has to stay that way. You can choose to faithfully reproduce a photo in a realistic fashion, or you can change it, either subtly or dramatically. Playing up certain attributes of the photo can make them stand out more. Pick a photo and think about how you could change one or more of the strongest features.

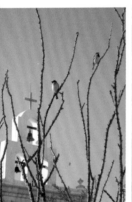    

Line

Color

Shape/form

Light/shadow

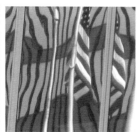

Reflection

Texture/pattern

Angle

Shoot a Mundane Location

Pick a place you think is going to be really boring, or a place you've been a hundred times without having thought, "Gosh, I should bring my camera next time!" Somewhere that is not visually interesting at first glance, or that is even downright ugly or uninspiring. Consider places such as:

- a construction site
- a playground
- your neighborhood
- a building
- a college campus
- a hardware store
- a graveyard

- a doctor's or dentist's office
- a city street
- a gas station
- a country road
- a grocery store
- a landfill or garbage dump
- a parking lot

Force yourself to look at this environment through fresh eyes. Look up, down, and all around. Explore. Look for interesting juxtapositions and combinations. You may even find unexpected beauty amid the ugliness.

A note about shooting inside stores: Many store managers do not want you shooting photos inside their stores. Trust me on this. I'm not sure whether they think you are a spy working for their competition, a thief scoping the joint, or what. If you want to take photos inside a store, ask the store manager for permission first. It doesn't hurt to bring along some of your work, or this book, illustrating what you are doing, and why.

All the shots on these 2 pages were taken at a mundane location: a rural church with a field behind it where my daughter's soccer team practiced. The charming red barn was in a field next to the churchyard.

Exercises

Challenge your assumptions. Think about the location you chose. Jot down why you thought it was boring when you selected it. Did you find interesting things to photograph? Did any one category mentioned earlier dominate (line, color, texture, and so on)? In the photos earlier, I anticipated that the church grounds would not yield interesting photos because they are not particularly attractive and because the facilities are somewhat dilapidated. But I came away with some great shots. Older buildings often yield wonderful textures (peeling paint, rust) and an evocative mood. Remember, you can take a beautiful or fascinating photo of an ugly subject.

Think like a photojournalist. Imagine you are on assignment to capture the essence of a location or event for your local newspaper. If you had to pick three of the photos you took at this location, which ones would you pick, and why?

Pick Ten Subjects and Shoot Each One Using a Long Shot, a Medium Shot, and a Close-up

A long shot shows the entire subject. A medium shot shows part of the subject, and a close-up shows only a tiny part of the subject. Think about the long shot, medium shot, and close-up shot the next time you go to the movies. Movies often start with a long shot that sets the scene and invites the viewer in.

If you look at most of the photos you are taking now, there is a good chance nearly all of them will be medium shots.

Because of their intimate nature, close-up shots are often better at conveying emotion, mood, and detail. They often also make good candidates for abstraction.

Some subjects will be strongest when shot in a particular way. This is partly a function of their size. (A butterfly is almost always best as a close-up, and if you are trying to convey the majesty and grandeur of a mountain, you really have to use a long shot.)

A giraffe is the subject of this study in long, medium, and close-up shots. The long shot is only ho-hum, although it does show the entire body of the giraffe, if that is what you need. The medium shot has wonderful pattern and negative space. The close-up is the most emotional and evocative of the three, and has nice texture. Which one is the best shot? It depends on what you are going to do with the photos.

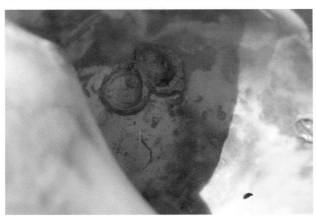

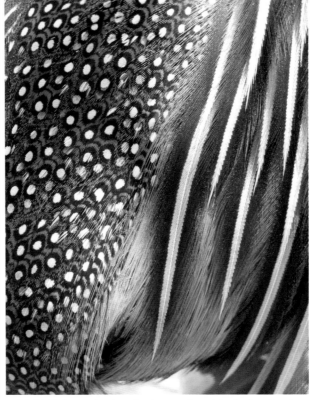

Different things stand out in this study of a collection of whelk shells on a picnic table near the beach. In the long shot, the planks in the table and the fence form pleasing repetitious lines. The strong colors and the form of the shell dominate in the medium shot. The texture and pattern inside the shell stand out most in the close-up shot.

This bird is interesting, but the close-up shot of the feathers has the potential to become a stunning abstract piece (see page 86).

Closer, closer, closer: If you are taking shots that show an entire object (such as the whole lily), get closer. Use your macro lens to get up close and personal. When you get pollen on your lens, you are close enough!

Exercises

Find out what floats your boat. Think about which shots you like best and why. You may surprise yourself and find that you are far more interested in one type of shot than in the others. Which one sets the mood best? Which one tells the story best? Which one pulls you in?

Use all the shots. Consider whether you could use two or three of your shots in a fiber art composition simultaneously. Cut and paste pieces of all three shots together into a new composition.

Using a macro lens reveals amazing pattern on a caterpillar, velvety petals on a hydrangea, and texture on a seashell.

Pick a Subject and Shoot as Many Examples of It as You Can, Aiming for Diversity in a Similarly Composed Shot

The object here is to discover the amazing diversity that exists in similar subjects.

Think about people, and the fantastic range of variation in hair, skin, and eye color; height; and weight. If you choose people as your subjects, focus in on one body part, such as lips, hands, eyes, toes, ears, or belly buttons. Then find people who will give you permission to photograph them, and shoot as many of these body parts as you can. This is a fun thing to do at a family gathering or with a group of friends.

Here are some other ideas:

- leaf forms

- silhouettes

- doors or windows

- tools

- pencils

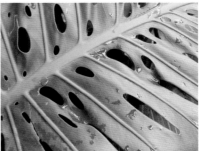

A collection of photos focusing on green leaf forms showcases myriad leaf shapes and textures.

When the subject is the same, a collection of photos may cause viewers to more closely examine the varying textures, colors, and lines.

Exercises

What stands out? Closely examine each photo and write down what you like about it (for example, "vibrant red color," "strong lines," "calm/peaceful"). Think about which shots you like best and why. Let's say you shot eyes. Are you drawn in by the intense color of the iris in one shot? Or do you adore the curve of the rim of the eye or the texture of the eyelashes? Or does it capture the essence or mood of the person? This will tell you a lot about what interests you and what you might want to turn into a composition in fabric and thread.

Make a grid. You are probably familiar with the posters, often sold in tourist locations, that feature "The Doors of Dublin" or some such thing. Take your collection of photos on a single subject and create a mini poster of your own. Try cutting all your shots to the same shape and dimensions (for example, squares or same-size rectangles) and paste them in a grid.

Same subject, different time. Shoot the same outdoor subject several times during the same day, the same week, or the same year. Try shooting a tree once each season, perhaps from the same vantage point. Or shoot a plant in your garden once a week from February to June, recording its growth and transformation from a barren stick to a budding, leafy shrub. Shooting a subject several times in the same day can be a study in how changing light conditions, the angle of the sun, or varying weather changes the look of the subject.

Shoot in Black and White

Most digital cameras have a monochrome or black-and-white setting that allows you to take photos in black and white (and see them on the LCD screen in black and white while shooting them).

People learning photography are often taught to start with black and white. By taking color out of the equation, you can learn a lot about contrast and lighting, and about paying attention to your composition and the forms and lines that make it dynamic.

You often end up with photos that are simplified and timeless, or with more emotion or drama. A black-and-white image can be more compelling, more stark, and more revealing than its color counterpart. Black and white is also great for capturing texture.

Photos shot in black and white may have a stark, graphic quality, or a nostalgic, old-fashioned feel.

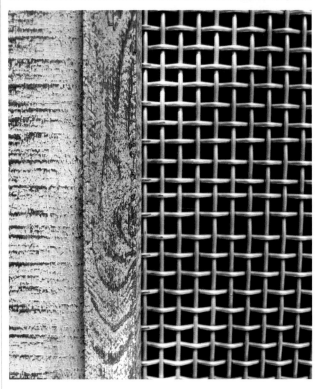

When shooting in black and white, try waiting until you have bright light, which provides lots of shadows and contrast.

If you can't take photos in black and white on your camera, you may be able to convert color photos to black and white afterward, using photo-editing software. Or try making black-and-white photocopies of your color prints.

Exercises

Slice it. Enlarge one of your black-and-white photos (either on your computer or on a photocopy machine) and cut it into slices. Paste the pieces back together in a different way to form an interesting composition.

Colorize it. Make a photocopy of one of your black-and-white photos. Use colored pencils or watercolors to color it, using hues different from the subject's original colors. Or color it monochromatically (using shades of the same color).

Flip it. Shoot a photo that is a silhouette of an interesting object. Eliminate the background (by either cutting it away or eliminating it in photo-editing software). Make multiple copies of it and experiment with flipping it or rotating it to form a more abstract composition.

For this composition, I silhouetted the metal palm tree sculpture and then flipped it in different directions.

The Next Step

Make a habit of practicing your photography skills as often as possible. If you have a small digital camera, consider slipping it into your purse, backpack, or glove compartment, so you'll have it with you when you see a great shot. Start building your own library of wonderful photos from which you can create beautiful art quilts.

The projects in this book are all based on photos I took over several years. I shot them in my backyard, in my neighborhood, at amusement parks and aquariums, at local farm stands, and at soccer practices. Even if you want to make art quilts from *your* photos, I encourage you to try working with a few of mine first. It's a great way to learn the step-by-step processes and techniques you'll need when you begin working from your own photographs.

GETTING STARTED

The projects in this book all use the same basic materials listed below. A few use specialized products (paint, Tyvek, Angelina, or fabric foils), which are listed with that particular project.

Supplies

Clear tape

Use clear tape to join the enlarged line drawings together.

Colored pencils, markers, crayons, or watercolor paints

I use colored pencils, markers, crayons, or watercolor paints to add color in the enlarged line drawing. This allows me to see what colors may work best for my piece and provides me with a guide for selecting fabric colors.

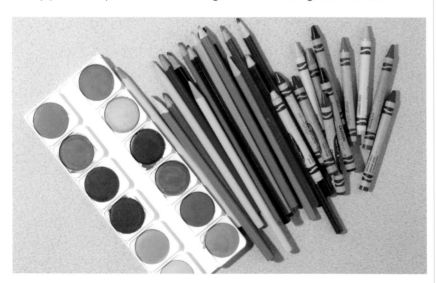

Cotton fabrics

Choose mottled batiks and hand-dyed fabrics, or small-scale prints. Avoid lightweight or sheer fabrics and fabrics with strong patterns or textures. Fabrics that look like the surface you are trying to emulate seldom work. For example, using a fabric with rock design for a rock wall may not be successful, because of scale or color issues.

All of the projects in this book can be made using fabrics the size of a fat quarter or smaller. The only exception is the background fabrics; some projects require slightly more yardage.

Backing fabric

This should be about 2″ longer and wider than the quilt top. Consider drapery-weight fabric; it can add desirable stiffness to art quilts and also acts as additional stabilizer during the quilting process.

Interfacing

Use Pellon 910 (a sew-in 100% polyester interfacing for feather-weight to midweight fabrics) or Heavy Weight Shaping Aid. These interfacings provide enough stabilization for your project while you are thread sketching your piece before you quilt it. Using lighter-weight interfacings will cause puckering and draw-up. These interfacings stay in the project when it is quilted, providing a desirable stiffness to the finished product.

Quilter's chalk marking pencils

I use mechanical chalk pencils by Sewline or Bohin, because they leave crisp, dark, fine lines. You may need different-colored leads for marking dark fabrics and light fabrics.

Clear upholstery vinyl

Use this product for creating positioning overlays.

Ultra-fine-tip and fine-tip permanent markers

Use black and a few other colors, such as red and green, for marking vinyl overlay.

Painter's tape or masking tape

I prefer painter's tape because it is easy to remove from surfaces.

Small sharp scissors

Use these for cutting both fabric and paper (on your fusible web product).

Lightweight fusible web

I like Lite Steam-a-Seam 2. This product works best for the technique taught in this book, because the glue layer is slightly sticky, which allows you to place and then reposition pieces as you work, before fusing them in place. This means that you can work on one surface and then carry your composition to the ironing board for fusing, and the pieces will stay in place. You can use Wonder Under or Mistyfuse, but they lack this important advantage. Avoid fusible web products with heavier glue layers; they can create problems for your sewing machine when you thread sketch your project.

Iron

Use for fusing fabric layers together

Lightbox (or bright window)

Use to trace original designs and creating vinyl overlays.

Transfer paper

Sometimes when a fabric is too heavy or dark, it is difficult to see the line drawing through the fabric using a lightbox or window. Transfer paper allows you to transfer the marks from the line drawing onto these heavier or darker fabrics. I like Saral Wax Free Transfer Paper.

50- or 60-weight cotton thread

I use Aurifil Cotton Mako 50 for thread sketching. To avoid puckering and draw-up, you need to use a very lightweight thread while thread sketching your project. Cotton is usually the easiest for beginners.

Low-loft batting

I use 100% cotton, such as Quilters Dream Cotton Batting in request or select loft.

Pins

Either quilters' safety pins or straight pins will work to pin baste your piece before quilting.

Cotton thread

Use for machine quilting.

Sewing machine

It must be capable of free-motion thread sketching and machine quilting. You will need to be able to drop the feed dogs, and have a darning or free-motion quilting foot.

Sewing machine needles

I recommend universal 80/12, top-stitching 90/14, or Microtex needles.

Specialized Products

Tyvek

There are two kinds of Tyvek: hard structure (slippery and looks like paper, but with swirly fibers in it) and fabric (softer, with more drape and subtle dimples). Either will work for the projects in this book. You may also use recycled Tyvek mailers. (Note: U.S. Priority Mail envelopes must be pre-used/recycled. It is a federal offense to use unused mailers for purposes other than mailing through the U.S. Postal Service, so you can't use new ones.) I used Tyvek in *Gourds*, page 67.

Acrylic paint

Any soft-bodied (the consistency of sour cream) acrylic paint can be used on fabric. Do not use the type that comes in tubes, as it is too thick. I used Liquitex Soft Body acrylics for two projects in this book, *African Beads* (page 63) and *Gourds* (page 67).

Angelina fibers

Angelina is a shiny fiber that can be found in a heat-bondable (Hot Fix) or non-heat-bondable (Staple) form. When heated with a warm iron, the Hot Fix Angelina creates a shiny fabric that can be sewn into art quilts. Hot Fix Angelina can be found in straight-cut or crimped-cut strips, or film. I used the straight-cut strips to create the shiny snow in *Snow Shadows*, page 73.

Fabric foils

Fabric foils are used in art quilts to add bits of sparkle. I used fabric foils to create the shiny web of *Spiderweb*, page 78.

Basic Instructions

Begin each of the projects using the following basic instructions. I have used *Indian Corn* (full project instructions on pages 40–42) as an example.

1. Use a photocopier to enlarge or reduce the line drawing to the size you need. For projects in this book, the enlargement percentage is indicated on the line drawing for that project. There are several ways to accomplish this:

Option 1
Take the book to your local office supply store and ask them to enlarge the line drawing.

Option 2
Enlarge the line drawing yourself, using a photocopier, repositioning the line drawing on the scanning bed until you can print the entire drawing. Then, tape the pieces together using clear tape.

Option 3
Scan the line drawing and then enlarge it using software such as Photoshop. You can also do this by placing the photo in page-layout software programs and enlarging it there. Print it out in "tiles," or chunks, and then tape the pieces together.

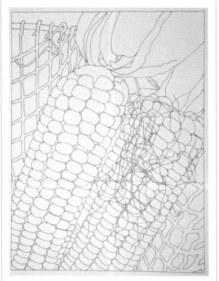

Enlarged line drawing taped together on back

tip If you use a method where you need to tape sections of the enlarged drawing together, make sure to tape your drawing together on the *back*, so that you can color the front without the tape getting in the way. To do this, tape on the front along the outer edges only (outside the outline frame); then turn the drawing over and tape it securely on the back.

2. Make the positioning overlay by cutting a piece of clear vinyl slightly larger than the sketch. Use painter's tape to tape your enlarged drawing down to a flat surface. Tape the vinyl down on top of it. Trace the main lines with a black fine-tip permanent marker. The marks need to be dark and fairly heavy, so you can see them through the fusible web. Make sure to trace the outer edge of the finished piece. Then, draw a second line ¼" outside this outer edge (this is your seam allowance). Write the word "top" at the top. (This helps you know which side is the front when you are moving and flipping the overlay.) Remove the positioning overlay from the enlarged line drawing and set it aside.

Marks that indicate specific details that will be done with thread sketching are shown on the drawing as dashed lines. In the case of *Indian Corn*, the outline of the kernels is marked with dashed lines, and for easy identification, the corn silk is marked with red dashed lines. Both the kernels and corn silk lines should be included on the positioning overlay, because you will need to transfer them to the fabric once all the pieces are fused down.

3. Using the project photo as a guide, color in the enlarged line drawing with markers, colored pencils, crayons, or watercolors. You don't have to be too precise; this is just a color guide. It is fine to change the colors. This is your opportunity to make the project your own—to add, delete, or adapt details you want to change. If the background is too busy, or not a color you like, consider changing it, as I did in *Papillon* (pages 46–48) so the subject of the composition gets more attention, and the colors pop.

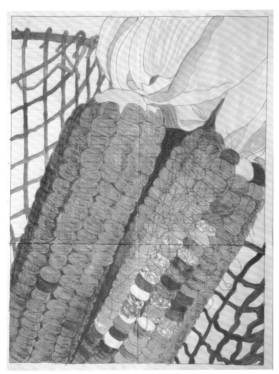

Colored with watercolors and crayon

4. Audition the fabrics you are considering. Lay them next to your colored enlargement and decide if they achieve the look you want and if they all work together. Remember, you can decide at any point to change the color scheme of your piece by using a different fabric. Make sure all your fabric colors work with the background fabric you have chosen.

Audition fabrics.

NOTE ....

I use a lot of batik and hand-dyed fabrics in my work. There are two main reasons for this. First, these fabrics are usually fairly heavy and tightly woven. This helps prevent darker fabric layers from showing through lighter fabric layers when the pieces are fused. If you prefer your fabric edges to look crisp, rather than frayed, batiks are a good choice because the tight weave helps prevent fraying. If you wish to use commercial cotton fabrics, make sure they are good quality and fairly heavyweight. I also recommend batiks and hand-dyed fabrics because they usually have nice mottling and color variations that will make your project look more realistic.

....

5. Cut a piece of interfacing 3″ longer and wider than the finished piece. See Supplies (pages 29–30) for details on recommended interfacings. If you have enlarged the line drawing by the size noted on the line drawing for each project, see that project's instructions for detailed size information. Note: Some projects in this book do not require the interfacing layer. Refer to project specific details.

6. Cut a piece of background fabric that is about 2″ longer and wider than the finished piece.

7. On the background fabric, use a chalk marking pencil to mark the outer edge of the finished piece. Then mark an outline ¼″ outside this outer edge (this is your seam allowance). Use a chalk marking pencil that will show up clearly on the background fabric. All of your thread sketching and quilting needs to stay within this area, so it is important to have a clearly marked line.

8. Position the interfacing onto a flat surface, such as a table. Center the background fabric on top of the interfacing and use painter's tape to secure the layers in place.

Layer background fabric on interfacing.

tip If you don't have a flat surface where your work can remain undisturbed during the time frame you will be working on it, consider purchasing a piece of 20″ × 30″ foam core (available at craft and office supply stores) and using it as your design surface. You can move it around and store it—either flat or vertically. You can also use the back of an old cutting board or a piece of mat board.

9. Take a close look at your drawing. Consider which fabric pieces will need to go under or over each other when you are building your project. In *Indian Corn,* for example, the corn husks go over some parts of the corn, and under others. The pieces should be layered from the back to the front. The wire basket goes behind all of the other pieces, so it should be positioned first.

10. Place the positioning overlay face down on the lightbox or bright window, so the word "top" is flipped backward. Tape it down.

11. Examine your fusible adhesive and determine which paper side has the glue stuck to it. If you are using a 2-sided fusible web product, such as Lite Steam-a-Seam 2, which I recommend, you will be drawing on the paper side that has adhesive on it and not the paper side that peels away before fusing. Do not remove the second paper side yet.

12. Place the fusible product on top of your positioning overlay, and trace the first element of your composition onto the paper side that has the fusible stuck to it. Work from the background elements toward the foreground. In *Indian Corn,* I first traced the wire basket pieces. Add a ¼″ seam allowance along each side that goes off the edge of the composition or that goes under another piece. Mark this extra fabric with a dotted line to remind you later where it is.

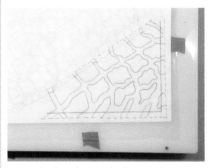

Trace basket piece with ¼″ seam allowance along edges. (Note solid and dotted lines.)

13. Cut each piece out of the fusible web, leaving about ¼″ around the shape.

NOTE . . . .

If you are working with Lite Steam-a-Seam 2 or another fusible web product with two paper backings, remember to remove the paper that does not have the drawing on it before you fuse it. If you forget, you will fuse the glue to both pieces of paper, and you'll have to trace and cut a new piece of fusible web.

. . . .

14. Place the paper side with the drawing on it face up on the wrong side of the fabric to which you are fusing. The sticky side that has the glue on it should be between the paper and the wrong side of the fabric before you fuse it.

15. Fuse the piece to the wrong side of the appropriate fabric, following the manufacturer's instructions for temperature and fusing time.

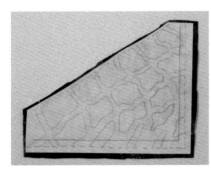

Iron fusible web onto wrong side of fabric.

16. Allow the piece to cool; then cut it out on the lines. Do not trim off the extra fabric you left for the seam allowance of pieces that go off the edge of the composition or under another piece. Keep the paper backing on until you are ready to start building your composition.

tip If you are working on an intricate composition, you may want to create only a few pieces at a time, and position them under the positioning overlay on the background fabric, before you create more. (See Steps 19 and 20.) It is sometimes helpful to number the pieces—both on the overlay and on the paper of the fusible adhesive piece—as you work.

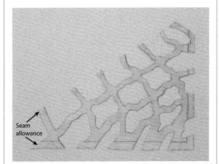

Seam allowance

Cut out, leaving extra for seam allowance (wrong side).

Right side

17. If you will be adding a lot of detail to a piece using thread, paint, or another medium after you build your composition, you need to mark these lines now. Tape the enlarged line drawing, right side up, to a lightbox or bright window. Place the fabric pieces on top to mark the dashed thread-sketching lines using a chalk marking pencil. If you can't see the lines well enough through the fabric, try making the lines on the enlarged drawing darker using a black pen, or instead of the line drawing try using the positioning overlay. Make sure to use a color that will show up on your fabric, and use a marking device that won't disappear when you iron the fabric.

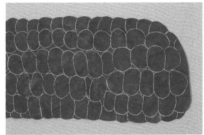

Mark thread-sketching details.

Using Transfer Paper In some cases where fabric is very dark or heavy, it can be difficult to see the lines on your colored drawing through the fabric. In this situation, I use transfer paper to transfer the lines. Saral Wax Free Transfer Paper is a great product to use because it leaves clear, dark lines. To transfer the design, position the fabric right side up on your work surface and place the positioning overlay right side up on the fabric. Then place the transfer paper, chalky colored side down, between the overlay and the fabric layer; then retrace over the lines on the overlay with a pencil. This technique is also necessary if you need to make marks on the piece after you have positioned all your pieces. (The corn silk in *Indian Corn* is an example of this.)

Transfer the thread-sketching lines for the strands of corn silk using yellow transfer paper after the fused pieces are positioned.

18. Place the positioning overlay over the background fabric, right side up, and align the seam allowance marks. Tape the positioning overlay at the top edge only. (This is so you can lift the positioning overlay to place the fabric pieces on the background, checking that they are correctly aligned.)

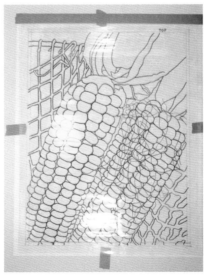

Tape positioning overlay across top edge, on top of interfacing and background fabric.

19. Remove the paper backing of the first background piece you want to position. In *Indian Corn*, the first will be the basket pieces. Position the first piece on the background fabric, using the positioning overlay as your guide. You do not need to be terribly precise, but try to get close. If you are using Lite Steam-a-Seam 2, you can stick the pieces down but still be able to peel them off and reposition them as necessary while building the rest of the composition.

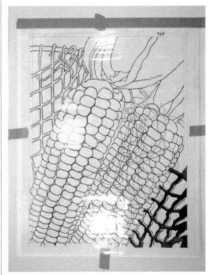

Position first piece under positioning overlay.

20. Continue in this manner, positioning pieces for your composition. After they are all in place, fuse them down, following the manufacturer's instructions.

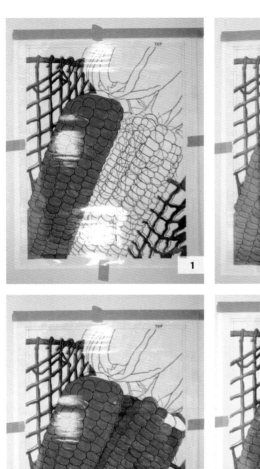

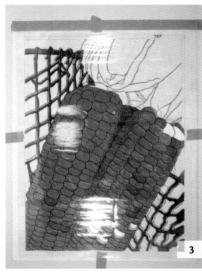

21. Decide if your piece needs more detail that could be added with thread sketching, and do this if desired. If you want to use a pillowcase-turn technique, do so before quilting. Or quilt your piece and then face or bind it.

tip It is sometimes useful to construct sections of your composition separately, off the background, and then add them to the piece. In *Indian Corn*, I did this with the corn husks. I started with the basic shape of the entire husk section and selected a light beige fabric that would work well as the base layer. I traced and cut out the outlined shape of the husks section from the fusible web, fused it to the base fabric, and then cut the shape from the fabric. Next, I removed the paper from the fusible-backed husk pieces and layered them on top of the base shape. After the pieces were positioned, I lifted the entire unit and moved it to the main piece.

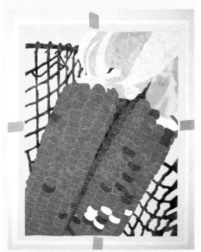

Position fabric pieces; then fuse.

REALISTIC PROJECTS

AGAVE GRANDE

Agave Grande, 20¼″ × 15″, Susan Brubaker Knapp

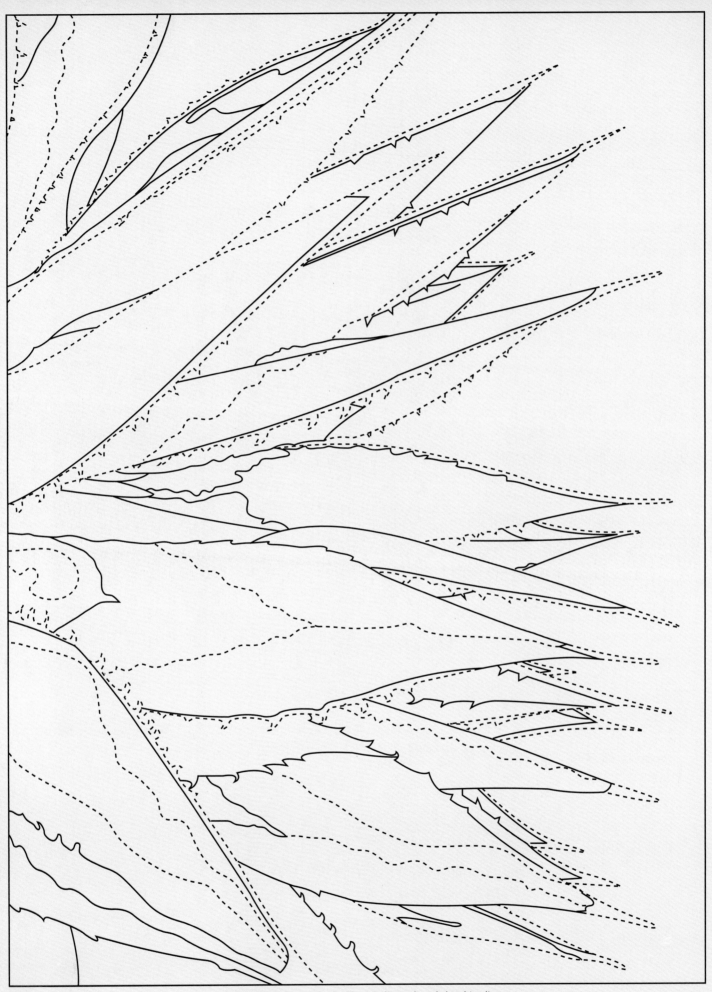

Enlarge 200%; 20¼" × 15". Dashed lines indicate thread-sketching lines.

FABRICS

- Blue background fabric: 22¼˝ × 17˝
- Interfacing: 23¼˝ × 18˝

Scraps of the following:

- Light yellow green (agave)
- Light green (agave)
- Medium green (agave)
- Very dark green (agave)

INSTRUCTIONS

1. Follow the Basic Instructions (pages 31–36).

2. This photo is very monochromatic, since it is a single plant. But the strong sun on the subject created striking dark shadows. I was able to create all of the agave spikes using 4 shades of green.

3. Many of the agave spikes have very subtle patterns on them that appear to be indentations from other spikes that pressed against them as they formed. After you cut out these pieces, but before you remove the fusible adhesive paper backing, place each piece right side up on top of the enlarged line drawing (also right side up) on a lightbox, and trace the dashed thread-sketching lines with a white chalk marking pencil or a regular soft-lead pencil. This will help you during the thread-sketching stage.

4. Position your pieces on the background, using the positioning overlay as a guide.

5. Double-check the position of each piece; then fuse down your pieces.

Ready for thread sketching

6. Using quilters' safety pins or straight pins, pin the background fabric to the interfacing just outside the marked outer edge of the finished piece. Pin every 3˝–4˝ in the interior of the piece.

7. While referring to the inspiration photo (page 37), stitch down your fabric pieces with 50- or 60-weight thread, adding details and texture. See Thread Sketching (pages 99–101).

8. Layer with batting and backing, and quilt. See Quilting (page 101).

QUILTING NOTES

Quilt around each spike and around the patterns on each spike. Quilt more heavily in the background, so that the agave will come forward. I quilted the background following lines in the mottled fabric.

9. Finish your piece with a traditional binding or a facing.

THREAD-SKETCHING NOTES

- If you examine the photo (page 37) closely, you will see that each agave spike has a thin ridge of spines along its edge. Since this ridge is so narrow, I decided to create it with thread rather than fabric. Stitch the spines using a light tan thread, following the thread-sketching lines.

- Add the patterns on the spikes with green thread, following the thread-sketching lines. Stitch vertical lines following the contours of the spikes to add depth and shadows.

INDIAN CORN

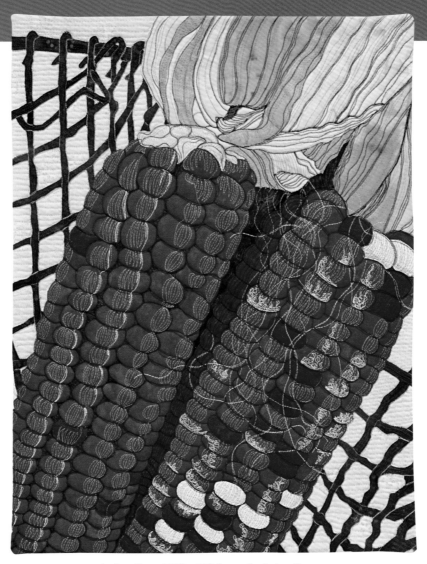

Indian Corn, 15¼" × 20", Susan Brubaker Knapp

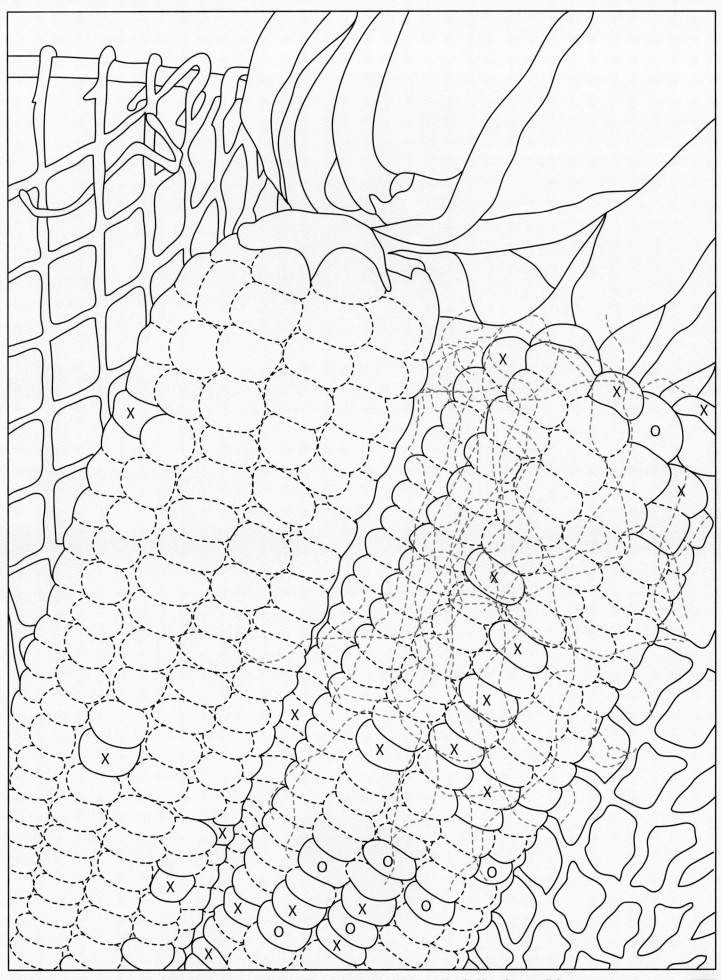

Enlarge 200%; 15¼" × 20". Dashed lines indicate thread-sketching lines (red lines for corn silks).

FABRICS

- Light yellow background fabric: 17¼″ × 22″
- Interfacing: 18¼″ × 23″

Scraps of the following:

- Red (corn)
- Dark red/maroon (corn kernels); *X pieces*
- White (corn kernels); *O pieces*
- Brown (wire basket)
- 3–4 shades of beige/light brown/gray (corn husks)

INSTRUCTIONS

1. Refer to the detailed directions and photos for making *Indian Corn* in the Basic Instructions (pages 31–36).

2. Position the pieces for the wire basket on the background.

3. Individual kernels of corn are marked on the corn fabric pieces before they are fused to the background and will be thread sketched later. Before you remove the fusible adhesive paper backing from the pieces, place each piece right side up on top of the enlarged line drawing (also right side up) on a lightbox, and trace the dashed thread-sketching lines with a chalk marking pencil or a regular soft-lead pencil. If the fabric you have chosen for your corn is very dark or heavy, it can be difficult to see the lines on your colored drawing through the fabric. Use Saral Wax Free Transfer Paper if this is the case. After the pieces of corn are positioned, transfer the lines for the strands of corn silk using yellow transfer paper.

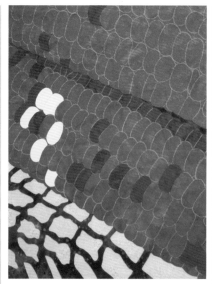

Cut individual kernels of dark red and white corn separately.

4. For the husk section, you can layer individual pieces on top of a light-colored fabric base, and then move the whole section to the main piece.

5. Double-check the position of each piece; then fuse down your pieces.

6. Using quilters' safety pins or straight pins, pin the background fabric to the interfacing, just outside the marked outer edge of the finished piece. Pin every 3″–4″ in the interior of the piece.

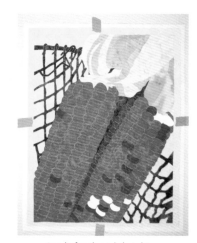

Ready for thread sketching

7. While referring to the inspiration photo (page 40), stitch down your fabric pieces with 50- or 60-weight thread, adding details and texture. See Thread Sketching (pages 99–101).

THREAD-SKETCHING NOTES

- Follow the thread-sketching lines to add the kernel outlines. Add shadows and highlights on each kernel with free-form stitching. Add definition to the husks with wavy parallel stitching.
- When the thread sketching is complete on the kernels and husks, stitch the corn silk using a light yellow or tan thread.

8. Layer with batting and backing, and quilt. See Quilting (page 101).

QUILTING NOTES

Quilt around the kernels and along the same lines you thread sketched in the corn husks. Then quilt around the wire basket, quilting more heavily in the background areas. After the piece is quilted, you may wish to hand stitch using a heavier thread for the corn silk, so it will stand out a bit more.

9. Finish your piece with a traditional binding or a facing.

RUSTY CHEVYS

Rusty Chevys, 20½″ × 15¼″, Susan Brubaker Knapp

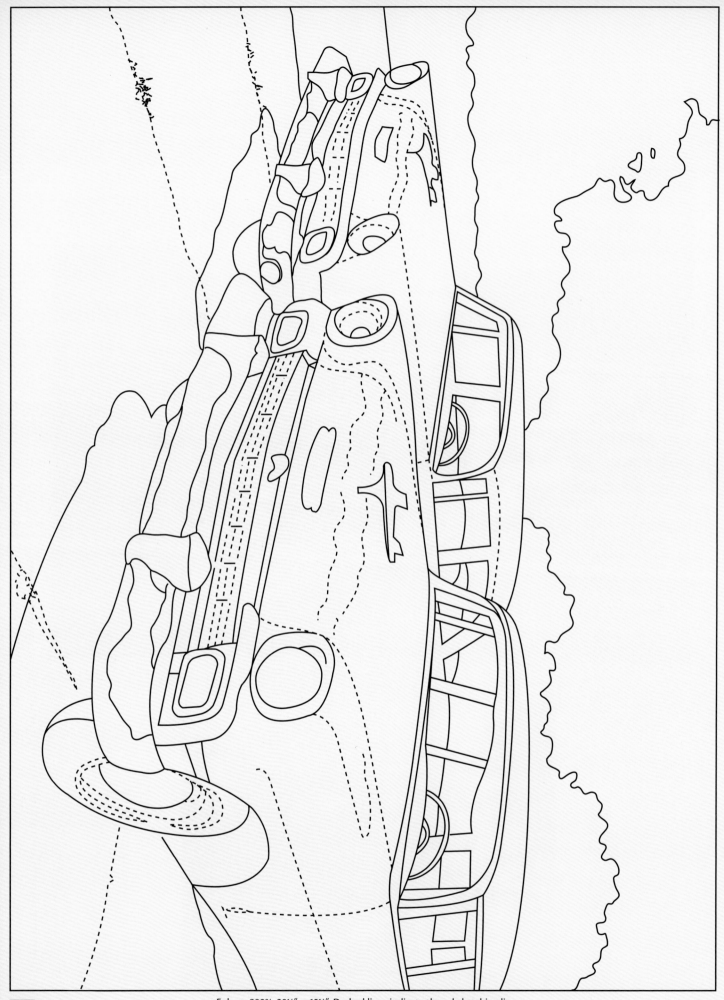

Enlarge 200%; 20½″ × 15¼″. Dashed lines indicate thread-sketching lines.

FABRICS

- Beige background fabric: 22½″ × 17¼″
- Interfacing: 23½″ × 18¼″

Scraps of the following:

- White (car, bumper highlights)
- Black (steering wheels, car interiors, tires)
- Dark brown (car)
- Medium rusty brown (car highlights)
- Dark brown/black (shadows under cars)
- Medium gray/brown (radiator grilles, car interiors)
- Light gray (car bumpers)
- Light blue (sky)
- Dark green (trees)
- Bright green (grass)
- Medium sage green (grass through windows)
- Dark sage green (trees through windows)

THREAD-SKETCHING NOTES

- Follow the thread-sketching lines to add car details and ridges in the road.
- Much of the charm of the original photo lies in the rust patches on these cars. You can create this effect by using lighter reddish-brown thread in these areas. Also note that there are a lot of dark brown/black shadows on the car in the foreground. The cracks in the pavement and the bits of grass in the cracks are all done with thread.
- On the two glass headlights, add the grid pattern and the rings of shadows and highlights.
- Using several different shades of gray thread on the bumpers and chrome pieces will blend the white highlights with the silver-gray fabric.
- If you used a strongly patterned green fabric for your grass, using different colors of green thread in a grass texture will make this pattern less distinct.
- On the windows, thread sketching horizontal and vertical lines with fine gray thread will imitate glass and tone down the colors of the interiors, as they would look if viewed through glass.

INSTRUCTIONS

1. Follow the Basic Instructions (pages 31–36).

2. Position your pieces on the background using the positioning overlay as a guide. Place the sky first, then the trees, grass, and car shadows. Complete the car interiors before working on the rest of the car pieces.

3. The car bodies, radiator grilles, and bumpers have a lot of detail that you will need to do with thread. After you cut out these pieces, but before you remove the fusible adhesive paper backing, place each piece right side up on top of the enlarged line drawing (also right side up) on a lightbox. Trace the dashed thread-sketching lines with a white chalk marking pencil or a regular soft-lead pencil. This will help you during the thread-sketching stage.

4. Double-check the position of each piece; then fuse down your pieces.

Ready for thread sketching

5. Using quilters' safety pins or straight pins, pin the background fabric to the interfacing just outside the marked outer edge of the finished piece. Pin every 3″–4″ in the interior of the piece.

6. While referring to the inspiration photo (page 43), stitch down your fabric pieces with 50- or 60-weight thread, adding details and texture. See Thread Sketching (pages 99–101).

7. Layer with batting and backing, and quilt. See Quilting (page 101).

8. Finish your piece with a traditional binding or a facing.

QUILTING NOTES

Quilting on the cars is done around each part, and in areas that should recede. Quilt more heavily on the background and in the car shadows and pavement.

PAPILLON

Papillon, 20″ × 13½″, Susan Brubaker Knapp

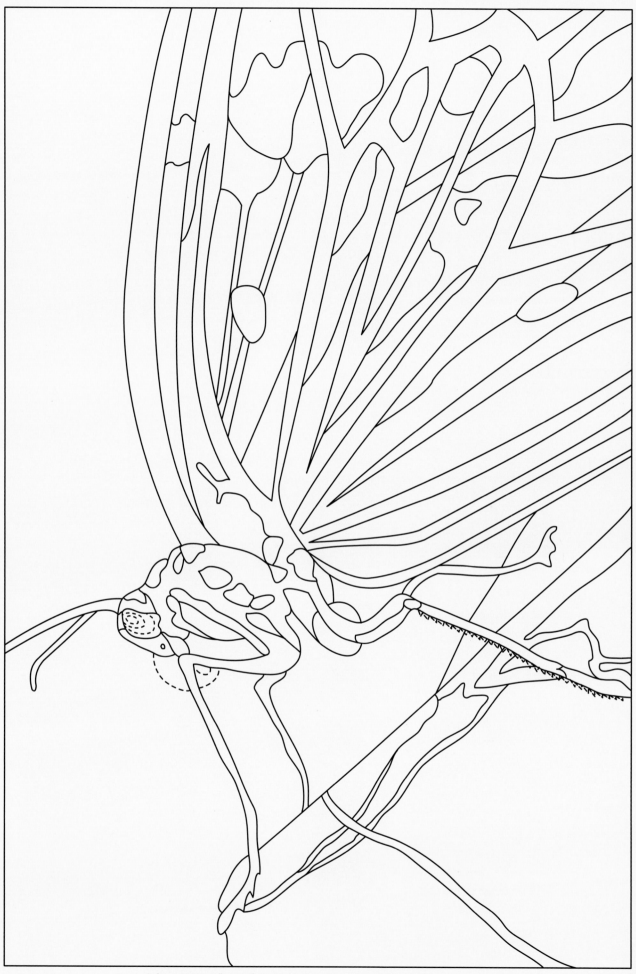

Enlarge 200%; 20″ × 13½″. Dashed lines indicate thread-sketching lines.

FABRICS

- Sky-blue background fabric: 22″ × 15½″
- Interfacing: 23″ × 16½″

Scraps of the following:

- White (butterfly's body)
- Black (butterfly's body, wings, and legs)
- Light sage green (leaf)
- Dark sage green (leaf shadows)
- Yellow (butterfly's wings)
- Chartreuse (butterfly's wings)
- Medium blue green (butterfly's wings)
- Light blue green (butterfly's wings)
- Very light blue green (butterfly's body)

INSTRUCTIONS

1. Follow the Basic Instructions (pages 31–36).

2. Position your pieces on the background, using the positioning overlay as a guide. Place the leaf and leaf shadows first and then the black butterfly body. Place the body parts, leg pieces, and wing pieces on top of the black body.

3. Double-check the position of each piece; then fuse down your pieces.

4. Following the instructions in Using Transfer Paper (page 35), transfer the dashed thread-sketching lines for the proboscis (the curled mouth part of the butterfly), eye, side of body, and hairy leg.

5. Using quilters' safety pins or straight pins, pin the background fabric to the interfacing just outside the marked outer edge of the finished piece. Pin every 3″–4″ in the interior of the piece.

6. While referring to the inspiration photo (page 46), stitch down your fabric pieces with 50- or 60-weight thread, adding details and texture. See Thread Sketching (pages 99–101).

7. Layer with batting and backing, and quilt. See Quilting (page 101).

QUILTING NOTES

Make sure to quilt along the edge of the butterfly to make it come forward. The butterfly will also be more dimensional if you quilt it less heavily than you quilt the background. Try stitching simple lines along the black portions of the butterfly's wings and body. I also quilted along most of the lines I had thread sketched in the blue sky and green leaf backgrounds.

8. Finish your piece with a traditional binding or a facing.

THREAD-SKETCHING NOTES

- Make sure to go over each piece, stitching it down along the perimeter. Follow the thread-sketching lines to add the proboscis.

- I used a flame motif to heavily thread sketch the wings and added a white netting effect around the circles on the wings. To create the hazy look of the legs and antenna on the far side of the butterfly, I thread sketched in a grid pattern on top of them. Don't forget to add the leg hairs using thread!

- In the blue sky and green leaf backgrounds, I stitched following some of the patterns in the hand-dyed fabric.

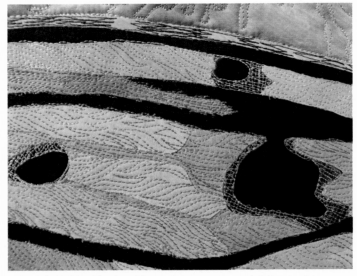

Stitch with white thread in netting pattern around circles on wings.

EXOTIC BEAUTIES

Exotic Beauties, 15¼″ × 20¼″, Susan Brubaker Knapp

Enlarge 200%; 15¼″ × 20¼″. Dashed lines indicate thread-sketching lines.

FABRICS

- Darkest green background fabric: 17¼″ × 22¼″
- Interfacing: 18¼″ × 23¼″

Scraps of the following:

- Medium green (leaves)
- Light green (leaves)
- 2 medium pinks (petals)
- Light pink (top petal in big orchid)
- Maroon (orchid centers)
- Cream/white (orchid centers and petal edges)
- Yellow (orchid parts)

INSTRUCTIONS

1. Follow the Basic Instructions (pages 31–36).

2. After you cut out the light pink petal and large orchid center, but before you remove the fusible adhesive paper backing, place each piece right side up on top of the enlarged line drawing (also right side up) on a lightbox, and trace the dashed thread-sketching lines with a white chalk marking pencil. This will help you during the thread-sketching stage.

3. Position your pieces on the background, using the positioning overlay as a guide. Place the green leaf background pieces first, and then the pink petals. (Use 1 pink for the main orchid and the other pink for the 2 orchids at the top.) Add the white orchid centers and then the maroon pieces and the white lines around the edges of the petals.

About the Small Pieces

For the small maroon dots on the centers of the orchids, it is not necessary to trace individual dots. Cut these dots freehand from a small piece of maroon fabric with fusible adhesive fused to the back.

4. Double-check the position of each piece; then fuse down your pieces.

5. Using quilters' safety pins or straight pins, pin the background fabric to the interfacing just outside the marked outer edge of the finished piece. Pin every 3″–4″ in the interior of the piece.

6. While referring to the inspiration photo (page 49), stitch down your fabric pieces with 50- or 60-weight thread, adding details and texture. See Thread Sketching (pages 99–101).

Ready for thread sketching

THREAD-SKETCHING NOTES

- After the pieces have been fused, the piece is still fairly flat. Thread sketching brings it to life, adding details, subtle color variations, shading, and dimension. This is especially true in the white-and-maroon flower centers and the yellow orchid parts.

- Follow the thread-sketching lines to add shading to the large yellow center and to add veins on the light pink petal. Add details such as the lines on the orchid petals by stitching parallel lines following the contour of the petals with a darker shade of thread.

- Add the subtle shadings and dotted details on the white and yellow orchid parts using contrasting thread. Add shadows and detail to the leaves.

7. Layer with batting and backing, and quilt. See Quilting (page 101).

QUILTING NOTES

After extensive thread sketching on this piece, the quilting acts mostly to hold the quilt layers together and to push some areas back while bringing others forward. Quilt around each petal, leaf, and orchid piece; then go back and quilt more heavily on the petals and leaves that are behind others.

8. Finish your piece with a traditional binding or a facing.

PINK CONEFLOWERS

Pink Coneflowers, 15¼″ × 15¼″, Susan Brubaker Knapp

Enlarge 200%; 15¼" × 15¼". Light gray lines indicate thread-sketching lines.

FABRICS

- Dark-green/black background fabric: 17¼″ × 17¼″
- Interfacing: 18¼″ × 18¼″

Scraps of the following:

- Orange (flower centers)
- Lightest pink (top petals in largest flower)
- Medium pink 1 (bottom petals in largest flower)
- Medium pink 2 (2 top flowers)
- Medium green 1 (leaves)
- Medium green 2 (leaves)

INSTRUCTIONS

1. Follow the Basic Instructions (pages 31–36).

2. The flower centers have a lot of detail that you will need to do with thread. After you cut out these pieces, but before you remove the fusible adhesive paper backing, place each piece right side up on top of the enlarged line drawing (also right side up) on a lightbox, and trace the light gray thread-sketching lines with a white chalk marking pencil or a regular soft-lead pencil. This will help you during the thread-sketching stage.

3. Position your pieces on the background, using the positioning overlay as a guide. Double-check the position of each piece; then fuse down your pieces.

4. Using quilters' safety pins or straight pins, pin the background fabric to the interfacing just outside the marked outer edge of the finished piece. Pin every 3″–4″ in the interior of the piece.

Ready for thread sketching

5. While referring to the inspiration photo (page 52), stitch down your fabric pieces with 50- or 60-weight thread, adding details and texture. See Thread Sketching (pages 99–101).

6. Layer with batting and backing, and quilt. See Quilting (page 101).

⊞ QUILTING NOTES

Quilt around all the leaves and petals and around the seed cones but not on top of them. (If you quilt on top of them, they will appear to recede.) Quilt more heavily in the background and on the flower petals that are behind other elements.

7. Finish your piece with a traditional binding or a facing.

◳ THREAD-SKETCHING NOTES

- Follow the thread-sketching lines on the orange flower centers to accentuate the seeds using green thread. Add the many small lines on the flower petals, stitching parallel lines following the contour of the petals.

- On the largest flower add a lot of shading with darker thread near the flower centers, where the petals are slightly shaded by the flower center.

- On the largest flower, at the bottom of the composition, you will need to add thread to "marry" the lighter-colored fabric on the upper petals with the darker-colored fabric on the bottom petals. Use some lighter-colored thread on the lower petals and some darker-colored thread on the upper petals.

- Also remember to use substantially darker thread on the two flowers at the top, so they will appear to recede behind the front flower.

- In the background areas, add details to the leaves and use scribbles of dark green thread and light green thread to make the leaf forms less distinct. The background should appear hazy and somewhat out of focus.

PARROT PEEK-A-BOO

Parrot Peek-a-Boo, 15¼″ × 20¼″, Susan Brubaker Knapp

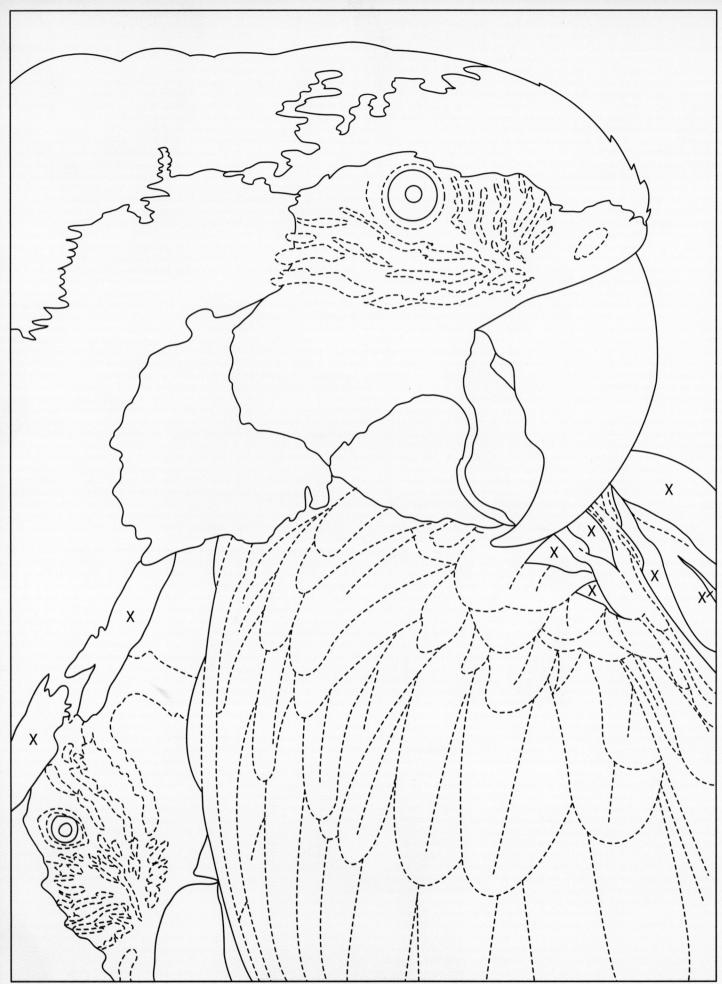

Enlarge 200%; 15¼" × 20¼". Dashed lines indicate thread-sketching lines.

FABRICS

- White background fabric:
17¼″ × 22¼″

- Interfacing: 18¼″ × 23¼″

Scraps of the following:

- Black (beaks)

- Gray (tongue)

- Darkest teal (chest of top bird and upper wing); *X pieces*

- Dark teal (wing)

- Medium teal (bottom right feathers)

- Light teal (back of neck on top bird)

- Dark green (lower left)

- Medium green (head of top bird)

- Light green (eyes)

- Medium yellow (bib of top bird)

- Dark yellow/orange (bib of bottom bird)

- Light blue (sky)

INSTRUCTIONS

1. Follow the Basic Instructions (pages 31–36).

2. In this piece, the white fabric for the parrot faces is actually the background fabric. Fuse the blue sky fabric at the top of the piece before you position the other pieces.

3. Some of the pieces—such as the beaks and some of the feather sections—have a lot of detail that you will need to do with thread. After you cut out these pieces, but before you remove the fusible adhesive paper backing, place each piece right side up on top of the enlarged line drawing (also right side up) on

a lightbox, and trace the dashed thread-sketching lines with a white chalk marking pencil or a regular soft-lead pencil. This will help you during the thread-sketching stage.

Adding Details on the Face

For the black areas on the parrots' faces, trace the lines from the enlarged line drawing onto the white areas and fill them in fairly heavily when you thread sketch.

4. Double-check the position of each piece; then fuse down your pieces.

Ready for thread sketching, with all details drawn on fabric

5. Using quilters' safety pins or straight pins, pin the background fabric to the interfacing, just outside the marked outer edge of the finished piece. Pin every 3″–4″ in the interior of the piece.

6. While referring to the inspiration photo (page 55), stitch down your fabric pieces with 50- or 60-weight thread, adding details and texture. See Thread Sketching (pages 99–101).

THREAD-SKETCHING NOTES

▪ You should add most of the detail to your piece at the thread-sketching stage. Examine the photo closely and add the feather texture, shadows, and lines on the beaks, eyes, and faces. Follow the thread-sketching lines to add the feather and facial details, and fill in the darker areas around the face with heavy stitching.

▪ Use a matching color thread and heavy flame stitching to add soft feathery details to the head and chest areas.

▪ Use a matching color thread and angular stitching to add the fine feather detail of the wing. Use heavier stitching and a darker thread to add the shadows in the wing feathers.

7. Layer with batting and backing, and quilt. See Quilting (page 101).

 ## QUILTING NOTES

Make sure to quilt around the outer edges of the parrots' bodies. Quilt more heavily on the parrot in the lower left so that it appears to recede. Quilting around each large feather in the lower right section will give the feathers more definition.

8. Finish your piece with a traditional binding or a facing.

GREEN BARN

Green Barn, 20″ × 15¼″, Susan Brubaker Knapp

Enlarge 200%; 20″ × 15¼″. Dashed lines indicate thread-sketching lines.

FABRICS

- Background fabric (choose any color; background will be completely covered): 22″ × 17¼″
- Interfacing: 23″ × 18¼″

Scraps of the following:

- Sky blue (sky)
- White (window frames, mullions)
- Black (window shadows, mullions)
- Dark brown (tree)
- Dark gray brown (dark shingles)
- Light gray brown (light shingles)
- Green (barn siding)
- Red/orange/yellow/green mottled (leaves), or use several different fabrics to achieve this effect

INSTRUCTIONS

1. Follow the Basic Instructions (pages 31–36).

2. Fuse the sky pieces to the background.

3. Some of the pieces—such as the barn siding and shingled roof sections—have a lot of detail that you will need to do with thread. After you cut out these pieces, but before you remove the fusible adhesive paper backing, place each piece right side up on top of the enlarged line drawing (also right side up) on a lightbox, and trace the dashed thread-sketching lines with a white chalk marking pencil or a regular soft-lead pencil. This will help you during the thread-sketching stage.

Creating the Windows

Position the sky sections of the windows first, followed by the black sections. Make sure to mark the reflections on the black fabric before adding the white mullions and then the white window frame. It is easier to do the mullions as separate strips, rather than cutting them out from the main window frame.

4. For the leaves, trace, fuse, and cut small sections of leaves and position them on the background. Keep working in this way until you are happy with how the leaves look. It is not necessary to follow the line drawing exactly. I used a mottled fabric that had shades of red, orange, yellow, and green in it, but if you can't find a similar fabric, use separate fabrics, and sprinkle the colors around until you are pleased with the effect. You could also use a single color fabric (yellow, for example) and add additional color when you thread sketch.

5. Double-check the position of each piece; then fuse down your pieces.

Ready for thread sketching, with all the details drawn on the fabric. Note that there is a lot of contrast in the sections of the shingled roof; adding color with thread will help "marry" these 2 fabrics, so that they will look a bit more similar.

6. Using quilters' safety pins or straight pins, pin the background fabric to the interfacing just outside the marked outer edge of the finished piece. Pin every 3˝–4˝ in the interior of the piece.

7. While referring to the inspiration photo (page 59), stitch down your fabric pieces with 50- or 60-weight thread, adding details and texture. See Thread Sketching (pages 99–101).

THREAD-SKETCHING NOTES

▪ You should add most of the detail to your piece at the thread-sketching stage. Follow the thread-sketching lines to add the shingle, siding, and window detail. For the window reflections, fill the thread-sketching lines on the window panes with squiggle stitching in white thread.

▪ Use thread to add texture, shadows, and moss on the shingles. Use vertical stitching to add detail to the boards on the barn. Don't forget to add details in the bark and leaves.

8. Layer with batting and backing, and quilt. See Quilting (page 101).

QUILTING NOTES

Quilt around the barn and then around individual shingles and planks on the barn to make them more three-dimensional. Quilt only lightly on the tree branch and leaves, as these elements are in the foreground and should come forward.

9. Finish your piece with a traditional binding or a facing.

AFRICAN BEADS

African Beads, 12″ × 12″, Susan Brubaker Knapp

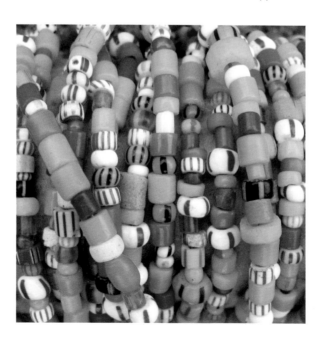

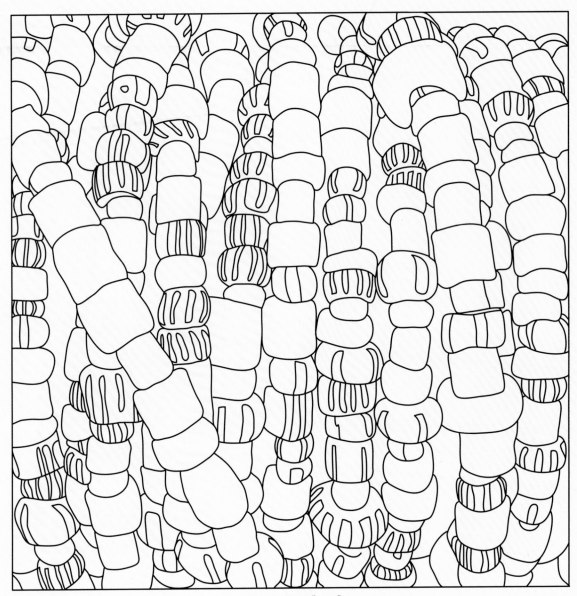

Enlarge 200%; 12″ × 12″.

SUPPLIES

■ Pimatex PFD (by Robert Kaufman): 14″ × 14″. This fabric is recommended for painting because it has a very tight weave, which makes it smoother to paint. It is also fairly see-through, which is helpful when you are tracing designs onto it. PFD, or "prepared for dyeing," fabrics have no finishing chemicals on the surface, which makes them ideal for accepting paint.

■ Interfacing: 15″ × 15″

■ A piece of foamcore larger than your project

■ Paintbrushes with stiff bristles with fine and very fine tips

■ Painter's palette to mix paint colors

■ Acrylic paint, such as Liquitex Soft Body acrylics, in colors you wish to use for your beads. I used the following colors: Naphthol Crimson, Titanium White, Hooker's Green, Phthalocyanine Blue (Green Shade), Medium Magenta, Burnt Sienna, Yellow Medium Azo, Yellow Oxide, Brilliant Blue, Ivory Black, and Bright Aqua Green.

■ Water

■ Rag or paper towels

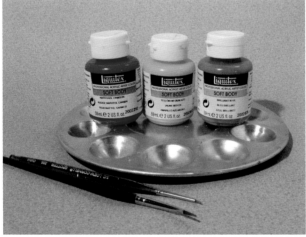

Soft-body acrylic paints, such as these by Liquitex, work well on fabric. A metal or plastic palette is helpful for blending colors.

INSTRUCTIONS

1. Follow Step 1 in the Basic Instructions (page 31) to enlarge the line drawing. For this project you will not need a positioning overlay.

2. Tape down the line drawing to a flat surface.

3. Center and tape your fabric on top of the drawing.

4. Using a soft-lead pencil, trace the outer edge of the finished piece. Draw a second line ¼″ from this outer edge. (This is your seam allowance.)

> *tip* Keep your pencil lines light but still clearly visible. You will be painting over the lines, but light paint colors such as white or yellow may not completely cover dark lines.

5. Trace all the lines in the line drawing, extending them out to the ¼″ seam allowance line.

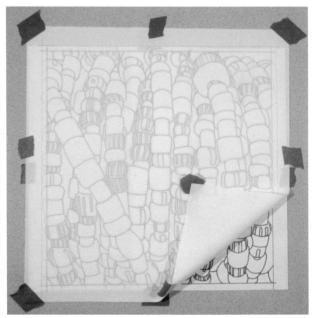

Trace line drawing and perimeter lines on white PFD fabric.

6. Take the fabric with the traced design off the line drawing, and tape it with painter's tape to a flat, hard surface on which you can paint. A piece of foam core works well if you need to have a portable work space. The paint will go through the fabric onto the surface below, so make sure that you can either throw it away or clean it off.

Tape fabric with traced design to foam core or another flat, hard surface before painting.

7. Squirt a small amount of 1 or 2 paints in colors you want to use onto your palette. Blend colors if necessary to create the colors you want to use. Work with a few colors at a time. Do not add water to your paint, as this may cause the paint to bleed out into the fibers of your fabric.

8. Paint in the basic color of the beads, following the photo to use the same colors I used, or choosing your own. Add shadows (by adding black to your basic paint color) or highlights (by adding white to your basic paint color). Paint the background black. Remember to extend the paint out to the exterior perimeter line (seam allowance).

tip Although acrylic paint can be washed off of brushes and containers with water, any acrylic paint you get on your clothing will be permanent, so wear old clothes, and use rags for cleanup.

Paint, adding shadows and highlights to beads.

9. When you are finished painting, allow the paint to dry thoroughly before stitching. There is no need to heat set the paint; it will be permanent after a few days (although washing is not recommended for art quilts using this technique).

10. Using quilters' safety pins or straight pins, pin the background fabric to the interfacing just outside the marked outer edge of the finished piece. Pin every 3″–4″ in the interior of the piece.

11. Layer with batting and backing, and quilt. See Quilting (page 101).

▦ QUILTING NOTES

Quilting is simple for this piece, since most of the detail was added with paint, and you don't want to quilt on top of the beads, or they will recede. Quilt around each bead, and more heavily in the background to make the beads come forward.

12. Finish your piece with a traditional binding or a facing.

GOURDS

Gourds, 12″ × 16″, Susan Brubaker Knapp

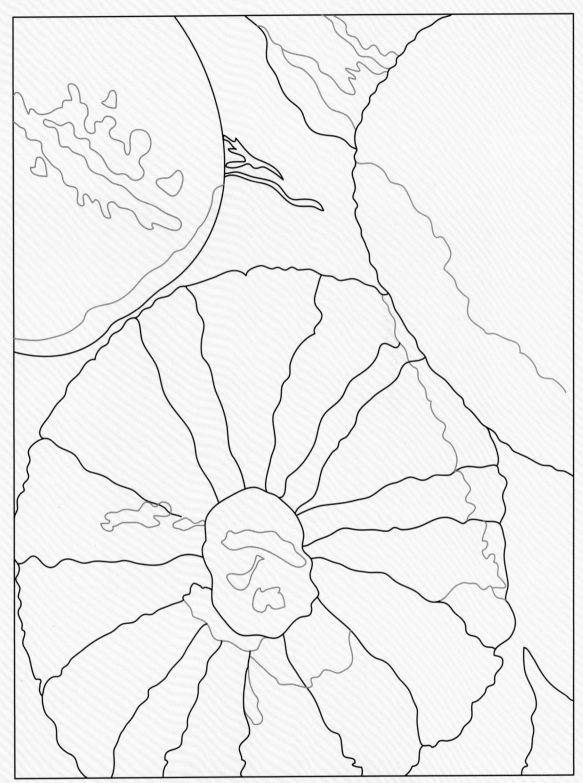

Enlarge 200%; 12″ × 16″. Light gray lines indicate areas of painted highlights and shadows.

SUPPLIES

- Black background fabric: 14″ × 18″

- Interfacing: 15″ × 19″

- Paintbrushes with stiff bristles with medium and fine tips

- Painter's palette to mix paint colors

- Foam brush, medium width

- Hard-structure Tyvek. Sheets of this type of Tyvek can be purchased from mixed-media online stores. You can also purchase Tyvek envelopes at office supply stores or use recycled Tyvek mailing envelopes.

- Metallic acrylic paint, such as Jacquard Lumiere. I used Halo Pink Gold.

- Acrylic paint, such as Liquitex Soft Body acrylics. I used the following colors: Naphthol Crimson, Titanium White, Hooker's Green, Burnt Sienna, Raw Sienna, Yellow Oxide, and Ivory Black.

- Parchment paper

INSTRUCTIONS

1. Follow Step 1 in the Basic Instructions (page 31) to enlarge the line drawing. For this project, make 2 copies of the line drawing, but you do not need a positioning overlay. Draw pencil lines ¼″ around the perimeter of each; this is the seam allowance. On both copies, number the sections in the largest gourd.

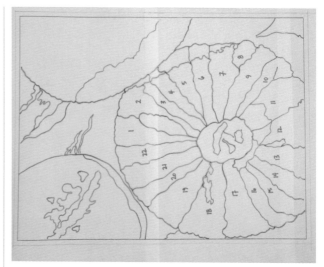

Number sections on big gourd on both enlargements of line drawing.

2. Place the line drawing on the lightbox, with the black fabric centered on top of it. Use a white chalk marking pencil to trace the outline and the seam allowance line. Trace all the lines in the line drawing, extending them out to the ¼″ seam allowance line. Pin the black fabric to the interfacing. (Note: If the fabric is too dark to see the lines, follow the instructions in Using Transfer Paper, page 35.)

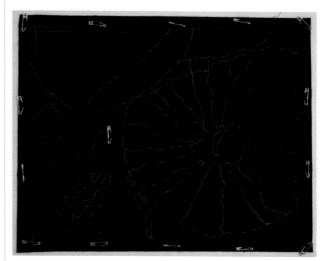

Use white chalk marking pencil to trace pattern onto black fabric; then pin it to interfacing.

3. Cut Tyvek into shapes twice as large as the gourd pieces. Paint the Tyvek with metallic acrylic paint.

Use foam brush to paint Tyvek pieces with a metallic orange-gold color, such as Jacquard Lumiere Halo Pink Gold. Allow the pieces to dry thoroughly.

tip The Tyvek pieces will shrink by almost half when heated. Each piece must be created separately because a Tyvek piece big enough for the whole gourd would be difficult to heat evenly.

4. Cut a piece of parchment paper approximately 7″ × 20″ and fold it in half to 7″ × 10″.

5. Place 1 Tyvek piece, painted side down, on one side of the parchment. Fold over the other side and place it on top of the ironing board.

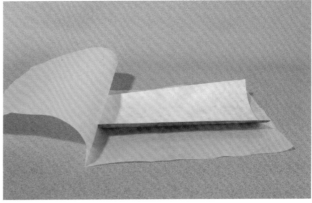

Tyvek will melt to your iron, so make sure to use an old iron and parchment paper on both sides of the Tyvek.

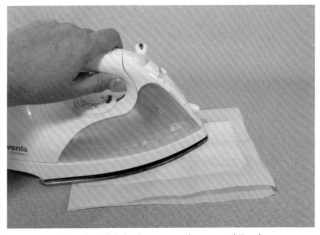

Hover iron lightly close to parchment and Tyvek.

⊞ WORKING WITH TYVEK

When you heat Tyvek, it is extremely important to work outside, and in an area with good ventilation. No extensive studies have been released regarding the possible toxicity of Tyvek fumes, and if you have respiratory sensitivities, this may not be a good project for you.

I move my ironing board out into my yard and set up my iron on a long extension cord. Set your iron on a high heat setting, but no steam.

Tyvek will melt to your iron but not to your fabric ironing board surface. Make sure to place the piece you are melting in between layers of parchment. This will protect your ironing board from getting stained with the paint and protect your iron from getting Tyvek stuck to it. Hover the iron lightly, close to the parchment and Tyvek. If you press down too hard, the Tyvek will disintegrate and have holes in it. Remember to place the Tyvek with the painted side down, away from the heat; bubbles form away from the heat source. Place the painted surface, on which you want the bubbles to form, face down.

6. Melt the Tyvek pieces following the instructions in Working with Tyvek (page 70). Pull the parchment back and flip the Tyvek piece so that the bubbles are facing up. If the bubbles are too high and you are worried that your sewing machine will have problems stitching over them, place the parchment back, and go over the piece (bubble side up) with a quick swoop of the iron, pressing down slightly. Do not hover this time.

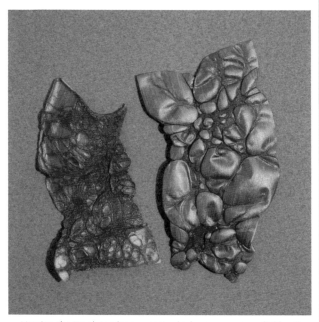

Heating the Tyvek too long or at too high a temperature (left) will cause it to shrink up too much for this project and form very small bubbles. Aim for results like the piece on the right. You may need to practice a bit to achieve the results you want.

7. Melt each of the Tyvek pieces in the same manner.

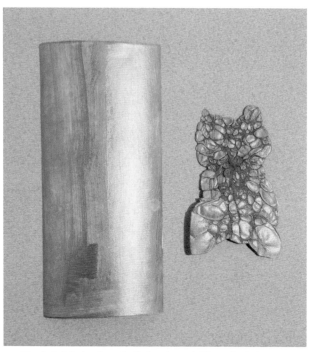

Tyvek shrinks by about half when heated. The melted piece on the right was created from a piece of Tyvek the same size as that on the left.

8. Take 1 enlargement of the line drawing, and cut out the pieces of the big gourd. Place each pattern piece on top of a piece of melted Tyvek, and cut around it. It is not critical that the Tyvek piece be cut exactly as the pattern piece, but they should be close.

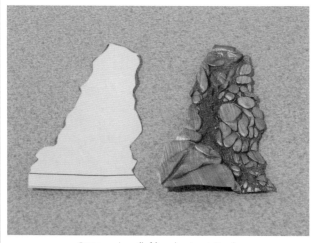

Pattern piece (left) and cut-out Tyvek

9. Position the first piece, referring to the numbers on the second enlargement of the line drawing, which you did not cut up. Hold the piece in place and stitch it down to the black fabric and interfacing. Use thread that closely matches the paint color.

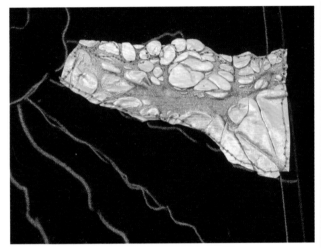

Position and stitch down first piece of Tyvek in largest gourd.

10. Cut each piece, and position and stitch each piece down, working your way around the gourd either clockwise or counterclockwise. In some cases, the pieces may overlap a bit, or leave a gap. This is okay, because you will paint in the gaps later. The remaining gourd shapes can be covered with Tyvek or painted (see Step 11).

The gourd takes shape when all pieces are stitched down. Note that a small amount of black fabric shows through the Tyvek.

11. Place your piece on a surface that will not be damaged by paint. Paint the Tyvek gourds and background with more realistic colors, using the photo as a guideline. You can allow a lot of the original paint color to show through. Note the highlight and shadow areas, and try to reproduce them as you paint.

Paint Tyvek gourds and background.

12. Allow the paint to dry thoroughly before adding any additional stitching. There is no need to heat set the paint; it will be permanent after a few days (although washing is not recommended for art quilts using this technique).

13. Layer with interfacing, batting, and backing, and then quilt the piece. See Quilting (page 101).

▥ QUILTING NOTES

Quilt most heavily in the areas that you want to recede, such as the lines between the gourd segments, the gourds in the background, and the black portions of the background. Remember that the stem on the main gourd should appear to come forward, so don't quilt it too much.

14. Finish your piece. I recommend a traditional binding for this piece, because the Tyvek pieces that go off the edge of the piece will not bend easily to the back if you use a facing or pillowcase-turn method.

SNOW SHADOWS

Snow Shadows, 15″ × 11½″, Susan Brubaker Knapp

Enlarge 150%; 15″ × 11½″. Red lines indicate the areas to be cut from the silver-gray Angelina.

SUPPLIES

- White background fabric: 17″ × 13½″
- Scraps of black fabric (fence)
- Blue Magic Hot Fix Angelina straight-cut fibers: ½ oz. bag (snow)
- Silver Iris Hot Fix Angelina straight-cut fibers: ½ oz. bag (gray shadows on snow)
- Parchment paper

About Angelina

Hot Fix Angelina looks like fluffy cotton candy or fairy hair. It comes in small bags in many different colors. When heated under the pressure of an iron, it bonds to itself but remains soft enough to stitch through. The color changes slightly if it is heated and may change substantially if overheated. Angelina is available from many shops that sell quilting and mixed-media art supplies and from online sources.

Angelina fibers are usually sold in small bags. A small amount goes a long way; less than a half-ounce of white and silver colors are sufficient for this project.

INSTRUCTIONS

1. Follow Steps 1 and 2 in the Basic Instructions (page 31) to enlarge the line drawing and make a vinyl positioning overlay. For this project you will not need interfacing.

2. Cut 2 pieces of parchment 17″ × 13½″.

3. Tape the positioning overlay down on a flat surface; then tape 1 piece of the parchment on top of it, and use a pencil to trace the outermost line (the seam allowance) onto the parchment paper. You will need to create a fused sheet of Angelina that is this big for the background of your piece.

4. Place this parchment paper sheet on your ironing surface. Take a handful of the Blue Magic Angelina (which is white with a slight blue sparkle) and snip it into pieces that are approximately 1″ long. Then sprinkle them evenly over the surface of the parchment in a thin layer. This will take at least half of a ½ oz. bag.

Use your fingers to sprinkle and sift Angelina fibers evenly on parchment paper.

5. Fill the entire rectangle, making sure that you don't have any bare spots and that the Angelina extends slightly over the lines you drew on the parchment.

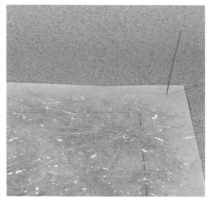

Angelina should extend over drawn lines on parchment.

6. Take your second piece of parchment and carefully lower it over the piece with the Angelina, so you don't disturb the fibers. Set the iron on medium-high heat. Pass the iron over the entire surface of the parchment, with a fairly quick, firm motion. Do not overheat, or the Angelina may discolor.

Press Angelina fibers between 2 layers of parchment.

7. Before you completely take the top sheet of parchment off, pull it back just a bit to peek and see that the fibers have bonded together. If not, put the parchment back and press some more. You may need to turn your iron to a slightly hotter setting.

Check to make sure fibers are bonded.

8. Once the Angelina has bonded into a solid sheet, remove both pieces of parchment and center the sheet on top of your white background fabric.

9. In the same manner, create a fused sheet the same size, using the Silver Iris Angelina. Make it slightly thicker this time; use about three-quarters of the half-ounce bag. The sheet needs to be nice and solid, because you will be cutting your gray shadows from it.

10. Place the white background fabric on top of your positioning overlay, and trace the outermost line (the seam allowance) with a mechanical lead pencil.

11. On your ironing surface, position the white background fabric and the fused sheet of Blue Magic under the positioning overlay, making sure that the Angelina slightly overlaps the seam allowance line. Pin through the overlay, Angelina sheet, and background fabric and into the ironing board along the top edge. This way, you can flip back the positioning overlay as you position and fuse the gray shadow pieces. A pin at the bottom helps keep the overlay in place.

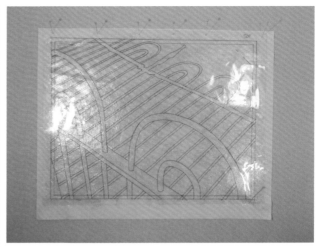

Position fused sheet of Blue Magic under vinyl overlay, on top of white fabric. Pin through all layers into your ironing surface.

12. Cut the straight pieces of the shadow from the longer side of the Silver Iris Angelina sheet. Measure the width of the pieces on your line drawing; then cut long strips using your rotary cutter. These strips range from ⅛″ to ¼″ wide. Cut them to the proper lengths, using your enlarged line drawing as a guide.

13. As you cut each piece of the shadow, place it on top of the Blue Magic Angelina sheet and under the positioning overlay. Check that it is positioned correctly; then pull back the overlay and pin each piece into place at the ends. Work from the bottom right corner, and only pin a few pieces at a time.

Position a few shadow pieces under overlay.

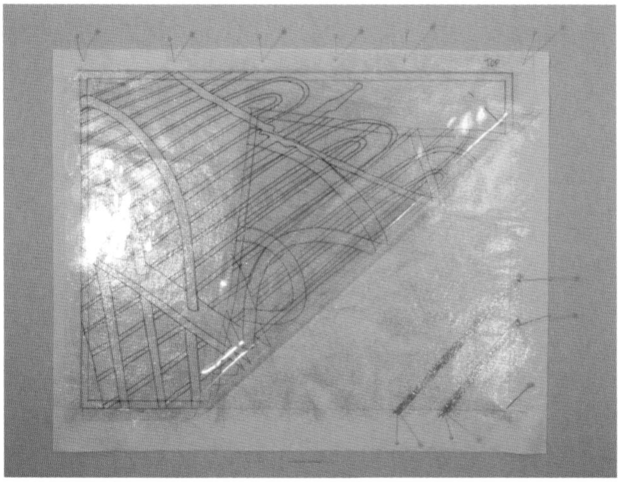

Pin strips of shadow at ends to hold in place.

14. Place the parchment back on top, and fuse the pieces down. Take care not to bring the iron into direct contact with the vinyl overlay or the Angelina. Then remove the pins.

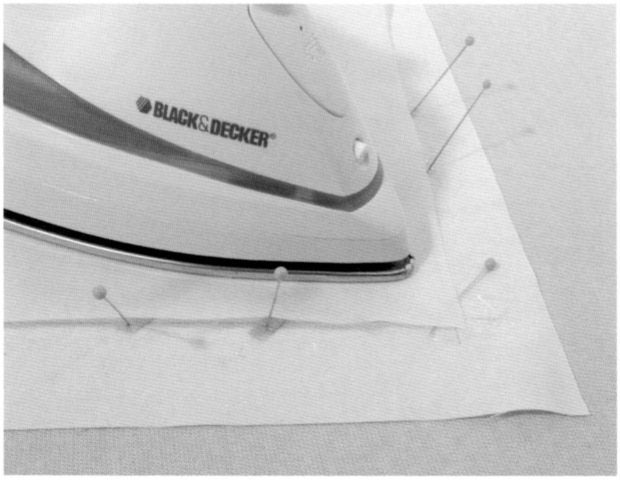

Fuse down Angelina shadow pieces a few at a time.

tip Angelina fuses to itself—and hot irons!—but not to fabric. If you get Angelina on your iron, don't panic. Simply let the iron cool, and then peel off the Angelina.

15. Keep working in this way until all the straight sections of the shadow are fused in place.

16. To make the curved sections, place your enlarged line drawing right side up on a lightbox. Place the remainder of the sheet of Silver Iris Angelina on top, and trace the curved sections using a black ultra-fine-tip permanent marker just outside the lines. Cut out each piece just inside the lines, so that the marker lines are not on your shadow pieces. Position each piece under the overlay, as before, and fuse into place.

17. The black fabric sections of the fence are fused to the Angelina with fusible adhesive. Trace, cut, and fuse them down as described in the Basic Instructions on pages 31–36. Make sure to fuse them under a sheet of parchment paper so your iron will not fuse to the Angelina.

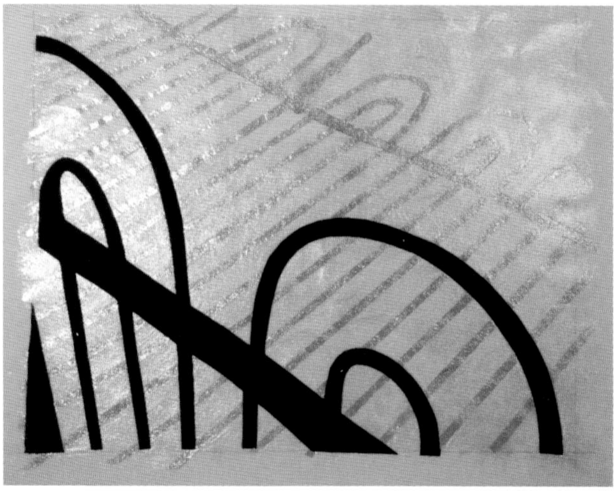

Ready for quilting

18. Layer with batting and backing, and quilt. See Quilting (page 101).

Quilting Notes

There is no thread sketching on this piece, only quilting. Use white thread to quilt around the shadows and the fence. This will help stabilize the piece for the rest of the quilting. Add white highlights on the black fence pieces. Blue-white variegated thread blends nicely in the snow areas, adding interest without calling too much attention to itself.

19. Finish your piece with a traditional binding or a facing.

SPIDERWEB

Spiderweb, 15¼" × 20", Susan Brubaker Knapp

Enlarge 200%; 15¼" × 20".

SUPPLIES

- Black background fabric: 17¼″ × 22″

- Silver foil sheets for fabric embellishment (spider web)

- Foil adhesive, such as Foil Transfer Adhesive by Screen-Trans Development Corp.

- Small plastic bottle with metal tip. These can be purchased at craft stores.

tip Fabric foils are a great way to add a bit of sparkle and drama to fiber art. You can paint or brush foil adhesive directly onto the surface of the fabric or apply it to a rubber stamp first. Another way to apply it is to cut and iron pieces of fusible web to the surface. Peel off the fusible web's paper backing, and then iron on the foil.

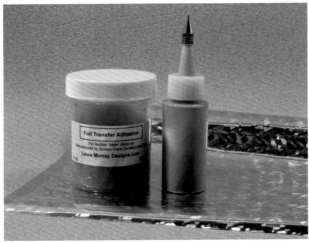

A plastic bottle with a metal tip, purchased at a craft store, is perfect for applying a very fine bead of foil adhesive to the fabric.

INSTRUCTIONS

1. Follow Step 1 in the Basic Instructions (page 31) to enlarge the line drawing. For this project you do not need a positioning overlay or interfacing.

2. Tape down the line drawing to a lightbox using painter's tape.

3. Center and tape your fabric, right side up, on top of the drawing.

4. Using a white chalk marking pencil, trace the outer edge of the finished piece. Draw a second line ¼″ from this outer edge. (This is your seam allowance.)

5. Trace all the lines in the line drawing, extending them out to the ¼″ seam allowance line. (Note: If the fabric is too dark to see the lines, follow the instructions in Using Transfer Paper, page 35.)

Trace line drawing and perimeter lines on black fabric.

6. Pour the foil adhesive into a small plastic bottle with a fine metal tip. Carefully apply a fine bead of the adhesive to each line in the spider web.

When applying foil adhesive, squeeze the bottle to maintain a steady, even flow of glue, keeping the bottle at 45°.

7. Allow the adhesive to dry thoroughly. This usually takes about 2 hours, but can be speeded up by using a hair dryer.

8. Place the piece on your ironing surface and position the foil, colored side facing up, on top of it. Iron the foil to the adhesive. Follow the manufacturer's instructions.

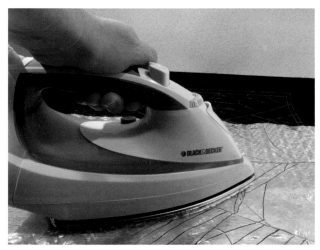

Fuse foil to adhesive.

9. Allow the foil to cool and then pull it gently away.

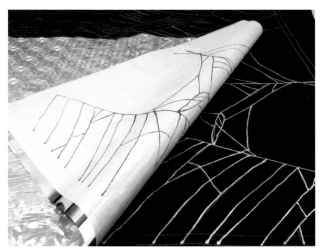

Foil should be fused to adhesive when you pull away foil sheet.

Ready to quilt

10. Layer with batting and backing, and quilt. See Quilting (page 101).

⊠ QUILTING NOTES

Quilt inside each of the web areas with a micro-stipple (a very tight stipple quilting design) and along the web lines to make the web come forward. I added a spider outline in one of the larger open areas.

11. Finish your piece with a traditional binding or a facing.

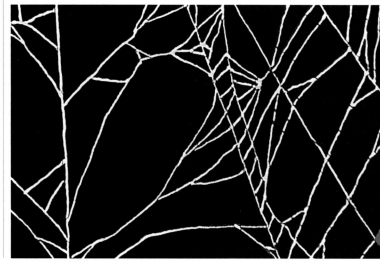

FROM REALISM TO ABSTRACTION

What Is Abstraction?

Abstract art uses the basic elements of art—such as line, color, form, and texture—to create a composition that is somewhat or very independent from things that can be seen in the real world (in a representational or objective way).

Even if you prefer working realistically, experimenting with abstraction can benefit you in these ways:

- Working in a different way, outside your comfort zone, will help you grow as an artist. You'll learn lessons you can take with you, no matter what style or technique you adopt.

- The process of abstraction encourages you to see things differently, to boil down things to their essence, to capture a subject's most intrinsic qualities, or to discover a strong mood or idea behind the subject.

- Abstraction can be used to focus attention on a particular aspect of the subject, either to make a point or to convey a particular emotion.

Ways to Achieve Abstraction

Abstraction is a spectrum or continuum. You can depict something in a fairly realistic fashion or take a nearly complete departure from reality. Consider a simple subject such as a red apple. Take a photo of the apple, and it is extremely realistic, although you have taken one step into abstraction by removing the third dimension. Next, render the apple by painting it on fabric. If your painting skills are fairly good, you can achieve a very realistic-looking apple. Next, try rendering the same apple as realistically as you can using fused fabric. The apple has now become slightly more abstract.

What next? Reduce the number of fabrics you use; this simplifies the color. Or streamline the apple's shape, making it less bumpy; this simplifies the shape. Eliminate the pattern or texture on the apple's skin. Keep taking these steps, and you will eventually arrive at a red circle, and then a black outline of a circle. The abstraction is complete; the black outline of a circle bears no resemblance to an apple, unless the artist tells you that it is an apple, or places it in a context that gives you clues to what it is supposed to represent.

To achieve abstraction, try the following:

- Simplify, change, replace, or eliminate texture.

- Simplify, change, replace, or eliminate line.

- Simplify, change, replace, or eliminate shape. The painter Paul Cézanne often reduced all shapes in nature to cones, spheres, and cubes.

- Simplify, change, replace, or eliminate color. Consider limiting your palette to just a few colors, or work monochromatically.

- Simplify, change, replace, or eliminate dimension. Altering the shading and highlights on an object makes it look flatter and less realistic.

- Simplify, change, replace, or eliminate the background. This takes the object out of context, making it less recognizable or completely unrecognizable.

- Zoom in close so the subject is less recognizable. In photography, you can do this with a macro lens.

- Zoom out, so that details subside and larger patterns or blocks of color emerge. Imagine yourself on an airplane, looking down on a patchwork of fields and mountains.

- Merge, rotate, or overlap subjects. What art elements change, or emerge as more important?

- Impose order and predictability on a subject with more random structure.

- Get random. Cut pieces apart and put them back together in a different way.

- Examine a subject for its deeper meaning or emotion. Then think about how you could convey those thoughts or feelings in an abstract way.

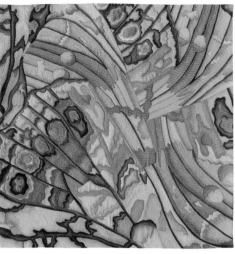

Lepidoptera, 39″ × 39″,
Susan Brubaker Knapp

Lepidoptera started with a photo of a painted lady butterfly on a daylily. Abstraction makes the subject of this quilt not immediately recognizable, and the piece has a sense of movement lacking in the original photo.

Detail from *Harbinger's Hope*, 53″ × 62″,
Susan Brubaker Knapp

The eggs in this bird nest have been simplified by limiting the number of shades of blue.

Cylindrical, 14½″ × 20″,
Susan Brubaker Knapp

Cylindrical demonstrates how to achieve abstraction through simplification of shapes and color values. The finished product bears little resemblance to the photo.

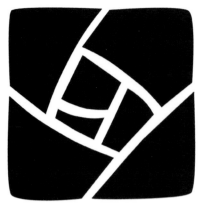

My interpretation of Charles Rennie Macintosh's Glasgow Rose motif simplifies the shape and imposes more order and predictability on the bloom.

Pink Rose, 8½″ × 8¼″, Susan Brubaker Knapp

The *Pink Rose* shows how greater abstraction can be achieved by reducing the number of color tints and shades from the original subject in the photo (upper left), highlighting the play of light on the petals.

Coleus, 7½″ × 11″, Susan Brubaker Knapp

Even though this extreme macro shot of a purple leaf was executed in a realistic manner, the result is a very abstract-looking piece. After I named and exhibited this piece, a gardener told me that this plant is not a coleus, but a plant called Persian hield!

Blue Feathers, 15¼″ × 20″,
Susan Brubaker Knapp

Starting from an extreme close-up (macro) photo helps create abstraction, because the subject is not easily recognizable. *Blue Feathers* started with a shot taken with the macro feature on an inexpensive digital camera. Since it is such a close-up, the elements become unrecognizable as feathers, and viewers are drawn in by the color and texture of the stitching.

Inspiration close-up (full photo
of bird on page 23)

Detritus, 18½″ × 13¼″, Susan Brubaker Knapp

Photos dominated by one or two art elements—line, shape, color, and so forth—are often ideal candidates for abstraction. In this case, I emphasized the strong lines in this photo of a brightly colored leaf by repeating the leaf and using unnatural colors. Choosing an unusual hand-dyed fabric for the background sets an "otherworldly" mood.

The next section of this book includes directions for four abstract projects. *Blue Feathers* demonstrates how you can take a realistic macro photo and create a very abstract piece. *Cylindrical* is an experiment in simplifying the forms and changing colors. In *Buttons*, shapes are simplified and used in a limited color palette. And *Detritus* manipulates a simple leaf form, repeated, resized, and recolored.

"Some painters transform the sun into a yellow spot, others transform a yellow spot into the sun."

—PABLO PICASSO

BLUE FEATHERS

Blue Feathers, 15¼" × 20", Susan Brubaker Knapp

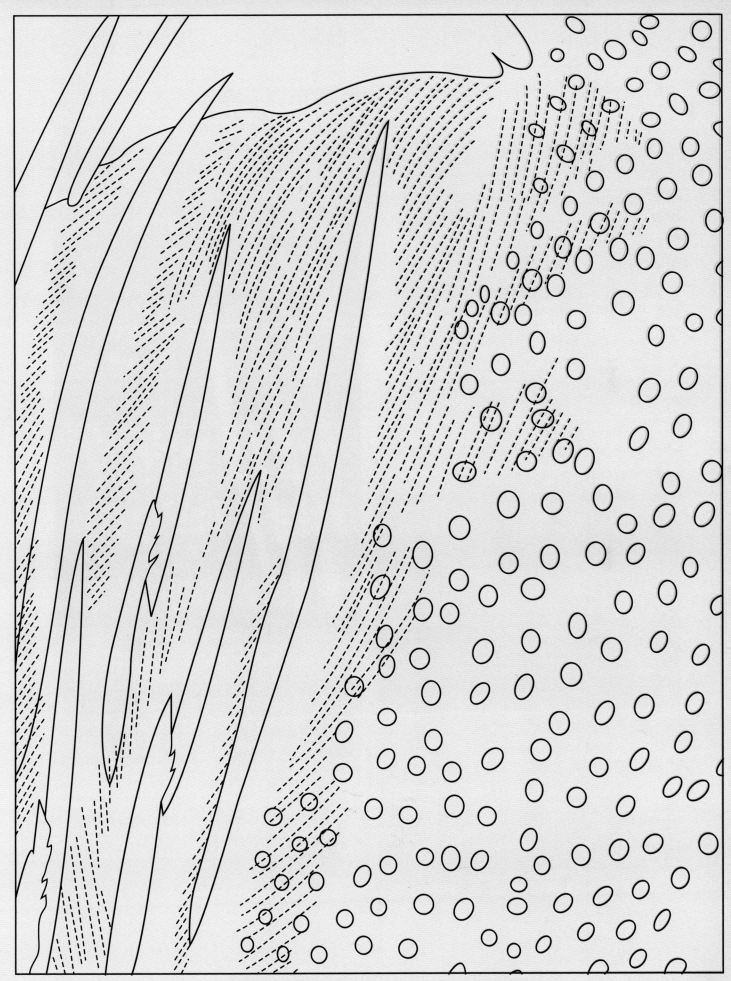

Enlarge 200%; 15¼″ × 20″. Dashed lines indicated thread-sketching lines.

FABRICS

- Black background fabric: 17¼˝ × 22˝
- Light blue or white tulle: 17¼˝ × 22˝

Scraps of the following:

- White fabric (stripes and dots)
- Green fabric (area at top left)

INSTRUCTIONS

1. Follow the Basic Instructions (pages 31–36). For this project you do not need interfacing.

2. Using a white chalk marking pencil, trace the outer edge of the finished piece onto the background. Draw a second line ¼˝ from this outer edge. (This is your seam allowance.)

3. Trace, cut, and position the green section, the white stripes, and the white dots. Fuse them to the background.

Cut out white dots.

> *tip* The small circles in this piece were not traced from the enlarged line drawing. They were simply drawn freehand on the paper side of a piece of fusible adhesive, ironed onto white fabric, and cut out. It is not important that the circles look exactly like the circles in the photo. Note that some circles are slightly larger or more oblong than others.

4. Place the black background with the fused pieces right side up on top of the enlarged line drawing (also right side up) on a lightbox. Using a white chalk marking pencil, roughly sketch in the dashed lines, which indicate areas where you will thread sketch in blue thread. (Note: If the fabric is too dark to see the lines, follow the instructions in Using Transfer Paper, page 35.)

Trace stitching lines onto background fabric.

> *tip* The thread work on this quilt is done during the quilting phase. I used black, blue, and pink thread to sketch my quilt, but feel free to substitute any thread colors you prefer to make the design your own.

5. Prepare your batting and backing fabric, and layer them in this order: backing (right side down), batting, and background with fused pieces (right side up).

6. Cut a piece of tulle about the size of your background fabric, and position it on top of the piece, pinning it through the background fabric, batting, and backing fabric, keeping it flat and taut.

tip If your tulle is crinkled up, place it under a piece of cotton fabric and press it quickly, at a medium heat setting. It will melt if it touches the iron or if the heat setting is too high, but will press nice and flat if ironed with cotton fabric on top.

Pin tulle over background.

tip Why use tulle? Tulle serves to hold small fused items in place without stitching on top of them, which can fray small pieces. As an added benefit, the layer of tulle acts as another stabilizing layer. Consider using it in art quilts where you need to tone down certain areas or subdue bright colors. Some tulles are sparkly, which can add a nice shimmer to a piece, creating an effect of water.

7. Quilt through all layers. See Quilting (page 101).

▨ QUILTING NOTES

Start by stabilizing the piece, using black thread to quilt around the white stripes and the green area. Do a few lines of stitching through the area with the dots; this will help stabilize this area, and the black thread will be covered up with pink thread later. Next, use blue thread to add feather details, stitching over the areas you marked with chalk. Use two shades of blue to achieve greater depth and detail. Stitch the area around the dots with pink thread.

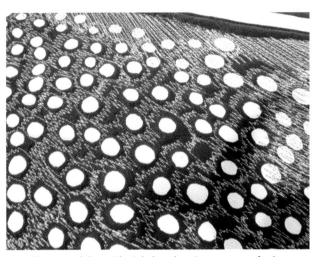

Stitching around dots with pink thread copies pattern on feathers, as shown in inspiration photo.

8. Finish your piece with a traditional binding or a facing.

CYLINDRICAL

Cylindrical, 14½" × 20", Susan Brubaker Knapp

Enlarge 200%; 14½″ × 20″.

FABRICS

- Beige or neutral-color background fabric: 16½″ × 22″

Scraps of the following:

- 7 values of the same green (See tip below for more details.)
- White fabric
- Gray fabric

tip This piece is designed on a five-step value system for the interior of the pipes. The fabrics run from a very light cool green (1) to very dark green (5). Fabric 6, used for the pipe exteriors, is a bright chartreuse that contrasts with the cooler greens in the interior of the pipes. Fabric 7 is a dark green for the darkest shadows and sky.

INSTRUCTIONS

1. Follow the Basic Instructions (pages 31–36). For this project you do not need interfacing.

2. Using a dark chalk marking pencil, trace the outer edge of the finished piece onto the background. Draw a second line ¼″ from this outer edge. (This is your seam allowance.)

tip Before you begin, you may wish to photocopy reduced versions of the line drawing and color each differently to see which version you like best. This way, your version of *Cylindrical* will look very different from mine.

3. When you cut out the shapes for the pipe interiors, note that you will cut the piece out exactly on the line along one edge and leave extra fabric on the other edge to be overlapped by the next segment.

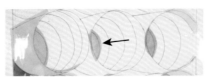

Fabric 5 positioned for center circle under vinyl overlay. Note how it is larger on all sides.

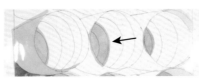

Fabric 4 positioned for center circle under vinyl overlay. Note how it is larger on one side and exactly on the positioning line on the other side.

Fabric 3 positioned for center circle under vinyl overlay. Note how it is larger on one side and exactly on the positioning line on the other side.

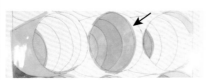

Fabric 2 positioned for center circle under vinyl overlay. Note how it is larger on one side and exactly on the positioning line on the other side.

Fabric 1 positioned for center circle under vinyl overlay. Note how it is larger on one side and exactly on the positioning line on the other side.

Some of fabrics 6 and 7 are now positioned on top of other fabrics, covering part of fabrics in circle (pipe interior) and defining its shape.

4. Double-check the position of each piece; then fuse down your pieces.

Ready to quilt

5. Layer with batting and backing, and quilt. See Quilting (page 101).

⊞ QUILTING NOTES

Your quilting lines can make the piece more or less abstract. Consider how the piece might look if quilted in a simple grid or with lines completely unrelated to the subject. Depending on the level of abstraction, people who view the quilt may not be able to recognize the subject at all.

6. Finish your piece with a traditional binding or a facing.

BUTTONS

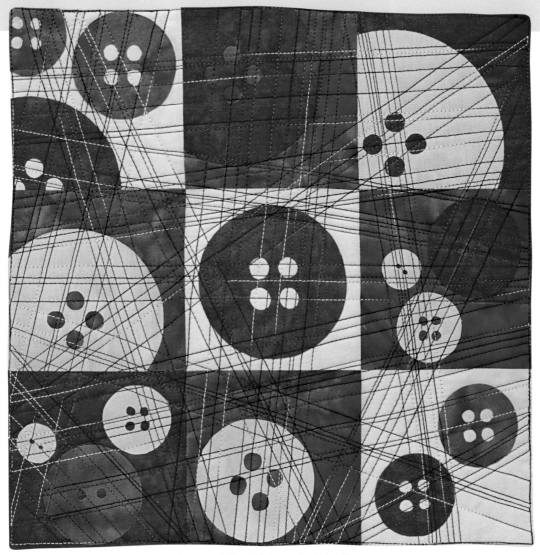

Buttons, 12″ × 12″, Susan Brubaker Knapp

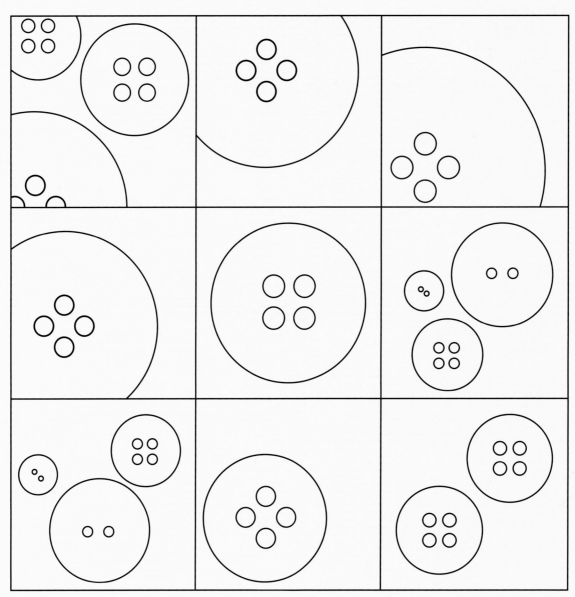

Enlarge 200%; 12″ × 12″.

FABRICS

- Background fabric: 14″ × 14″

Scraps of the following:

- Red
- Yellow
- Blue

INSTRUCTIONS

1. Follow Step 1 in the Basic Instructions (page 31) to enlarge the line drawing. For this project you will not need a positioning overlay or interfacing.

2. Cut 4 blue squares 4½″ × 4½″, 3 yellow squares 4½″ × 4½″, and 2 red squares 4½″ × 4½″.

tip There is no need to create a positioning overlay for this piece; exact placement of the button shapes is unimportant.

3. Place the enlarged line drawing on a lightbox or bright window, wrong side up. Trace the button shapes on fusible adhesive, making sure to leave the ¼″ seam allowance where the button shapes go off the edge of the square. Place them on the wrong side of the appropriate fabrics, and fuse them.

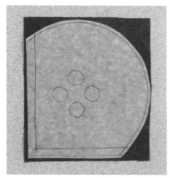

Trace and fuse button shapes.

4. Cut out all the button shapes and position them on the squares, using the photo of the finished quilt for color reference. Fuse them to the squares.

Fuse button shapes to squares.

5. Sew the squares together in rows, using a ¼″ seam. Press the seams open to reduce bulk from the fusible adhesive.

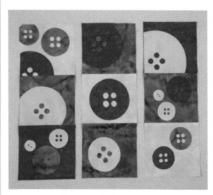

Sew blocks into rows.

6. Sew the rows together, carefully matching seams. Press the seams open.

Ready to quilt

7. Layer with batting and backing, and quilt. See Quilting (page 101).

▨ QUILTING NOTES

Quilting in concentric circles (echo quilting) will help emphasize the circular buttons, but this piece could be quilted in any number of ways. You might consider using perle cotton or yarn to hand stitch X shapes through the holes in the buttons, just as you would sew on a real button.

8. Finish your piece with a traditional binding or a facing.

DETRITUS

Detritus, 18½″ × 13¼″, Susan Brubaker Knapp

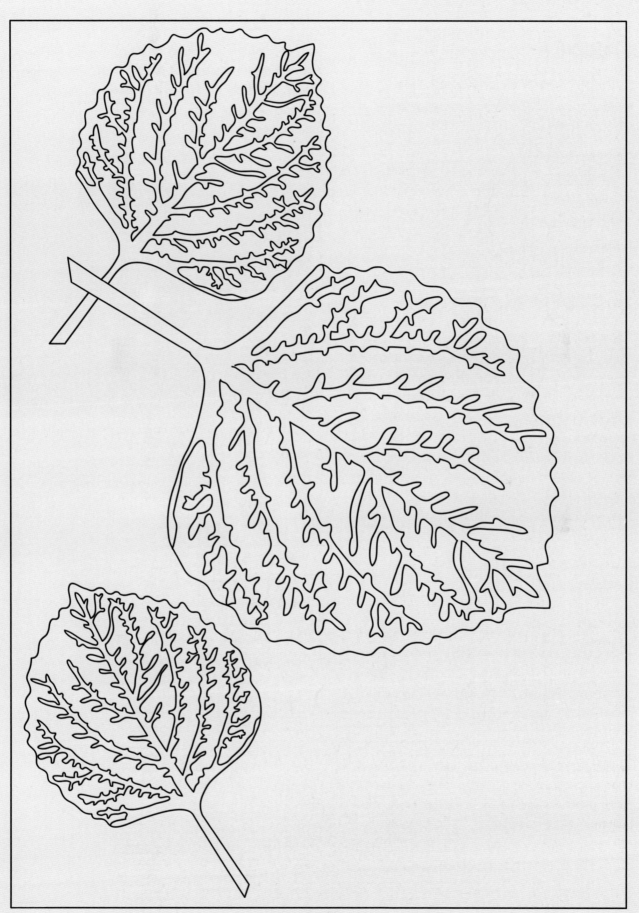

Enlarge 200%; 18½″ × 13¼″.

FABRICS

- Hand-dyed background fabric: 23½″ × 18¼″

Scraps of the following brightly colored batiks or hand-dyed fabrics:

- Chartreuse (leaves)
- Orange (leaves)
- Yellow (leaves)
- Maroon (veins)
- Blue (veins)
- Pink (veins)

INSTRUCTIONS

1. Follow the Basic Instructions (pages 31–36). You can make a positioning overlay for this project or simply position the leaves by eye. For this project you do not need interfacing. When you draw your chalk outline, position it in the center of the background fabric. You may wish to use the fabric at the sides and top of your piece in your final composition. The chalk outline will help you position the leaves as they are shown in the line drawing. You'll add the leaf scraps and quilted leaves later and determine the final size of your piece depending on them.

2. Position the leaf backgrounds first; then cut and position the veins.

> **tip** It takes a long time to cut out the intricate veins. Use a small pair of very sharp scissors to get into the nooks and crannies. Try to preserve large sections intact; you will use these for the scattered pieces at the bottom of the piece.

3. Place the enlarged line drawing on a lightbox or bright window, wrong side up. Trace the leaves on your background in a way that looks natural to you. You will quilt these leaf designs later.

4. Position the sections of the veins that you cut away at the bottom of the piece. Scatter them, and arrange them so that they are pleasing to the eye. The effect should be that of leaves and leaf fragments fallen to the forest floor.

5. Fuse the shapes to the background.

Fuse all pieces down, and clearly mark leaves that will be quilted into background with chalk marking pencil.

6. Layer with batting and backing, and quilt. See Quilting (page 101).

▨ QUILTING NOTES

Consider using thread that will contrast with the colors of the leaves, veins, and background. Variegated threads or threads in other bright, unnatural colors will add interest. Quilting the background with thread that closely matches it will help the leaves to stand out more. I transferred the outline of the leaves onto the background and quilted the design to add an additional design layer.

7. Finish your piece with a traditional binding or a facing.

Thread Sketching

Thread sketching is machine stitching with thread on the surface of a piece to add detail. It is done only through the top layer of an art quilt and the stabilizer, before the batting is added and the piece is quilted. Thread painting is much heavier—what I consider free-motion machine embroidery.

Thread sketching is much more than just stitching down the fused pieces, although that is an important function. It is the perfect way to add details to your piece—shadows, highlights, subtle color variations, and texture. With thread sketching, your piece will go from flat and uninspiring to a work of art that looks completely alive.

Thread Weights

When you start thread sketching a piece, always begin with very lightweight thread, such as a 40-, 50-, or 60-weight. Cotton is easiest for beginners. Lighter threads have higher numbers (60), and heavy threads have lower ones (12).

Thread weight is an important consideration in thread sketching. Always begin with very lightweight thread and work your way up to heavier threads, or you will have problems with puckering and draw-up. I save heavier-weight threads for the quilting phase.

Thread Types

Cotton is the easiest thread to use if you are a beginner, and is the type I use almost exclusively. But if you are trying to create the effect of a shiny surface, consider silk or polyester.

Tension Issues

Expect to spend some time initially finding the right tension settings for your machine. These settings will need to be changed if any of the variables (quilt thickness, quilt materials, thread type or weight, stabilizer, etc.) change.

Needles

Use a new needle, and consider what you are stitching through. The needle's size, sharpness, and point type are very important. The needles that work best for thread sketching are universal 80/12, top-stitching 90/14, and Microtex.

Helpful Products

Quilting gloves such as Grabaroos (by File Gloves Plus) have rubber tips that help you grip the surface of the quilt while you thread sketch and quilt. Placing a Teflon sheet such as the Supreme Free-Motion Slider (by Pat LaPierre) on the bed of your sewing machine helps your quilt slide smoothly as you machine stitch.

Stabilizer

If you don't stabilize your work before you begin thread sketching, you will be very frustrated and have poor results. Using a fairly heavy stabilizer seems foreign to those who come to art quilting from a traditional quilting background, where you want your quilt to be soft and flexible. In art quilts, a heavy stabilizer is desirable, because it will help your piece lie flat and hang properly on the wall. The two products I use most are nonfusible, nonwoven interfacings: Pellon 910 or Heavy Weight Shaping Aid. Lighter products will not give you good results. In fact, I sometimes use two layers of heavy interfacing to stabilize my work, especially if there are not a lot of fused pieces on the quilt top.

To Hoop or Not to Hoop

I really hate to use a hoop; I think hoops take too much time to put on and take off, and they limit my mobility when stitching a piece. So I have developed a method of working that doesn't use one. But a hoop might work great for you. Or you might try something like Quilt Halo (by Sharon Schamber), a heavy metal ring with a rubber bottom that sits on top of the quilt but can be slid around as you move from one area to the next.

Work Space Issues and Materials

You will see great improvement in your work by working with your machine set down into a cabinet, by giving yourself a large flat work space, by having your machine in good working order, and by paying attention to ergonomics.

Machine Basics

Most newer sewing machines are capable of doing thread sketching. You need to be able to drop or cover the feed dogs (the little teeth under the needle), and you need a special presser foot that will allow you to see where you are working. These are usually the feet designed for free-motion machine quilting or darning, and are circular or oval metal or acrylic feet.

How to Work

Always try to cover a lot of ground, and don't work in any one area too much. Aim to remove all your pins and do some stitching across the entire surface of your piece before you go back and add more detail. Start with very lightweight thread, so your piece does not draw up and pucker. Use heavier threads near the end of your thread sketching, or use them during the quilting phase.

Think carefully about the effect you are trying to achieve, and stitch that way. Your lines of stitching may be long and flowing, short and jagged, or smooth and languid.

Detail from *Maximum Cat Nap*, 22″ × 18½″, Susan Brubaker Knapp

To create the effect of realistic cat fur like that shown in the photo on which this piece is based, I used very fine thread and short, jagged lines of stitching that overlapped, and I changed direction slightly every so often.

Quilting

The art quilts in this book are free-motion machine-quilted. After the thread sketching, there is often little need for extensive quilting, except to hold the layers together and to make some elements recede and others come forward.

Thread sketching adds two-dimensional definition; the thread can be used to add shadows and highlights that make the elements more dimensional. But quilting adds three-dimensional definition; the elements will physically come forward or backward, depending on how heavily you quilt them.

Red Coleus, 11¾" × 11¾",
Susan Brubaker Knapp

The amount of thread sketching needed depends on the subject. In this piece, so much of the detail was added when the piece was painted that it required little thread sketching or quilting.

Detail from *Autumn's Bounty*, 12" × 12",
Susan Brubaker Knapp

I heavily thread sketched the pumpkins in this piece to add texture before quilting, but only along the ridges and around the pumpkins themselves. A little extra batting under the pumpkins in the foreground makes them appear to come forward even more.

Round Red Barn, 14" × 19",
Susan Brubaker Knapp

Quilting on top of the thread-sketched lines around the stones in the foundation of the barn helps the individual stones come forward.

Detail from *The Bluest Eye*, 12" × 12",
Susan Brubaker Knapp

The eyelashes on this small piece were too fine to create in fabric, so they had to be stitched with thread.

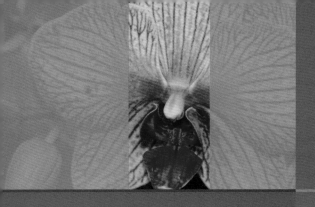

In 2009, a small fiber art group to which I belong decided to create works for an exhibition based on photographs we had taken of orchids at our local botanical garden. The three pieces on this page are all results of this venture and demonstrate how each artist's style shines through, despite the similar subject.

Blue Orchid, 23″ × 30″, Linda Stegall

Orchids for Andy, 12″ × 18″, by Deborah Langsam

Tightrope Walker, 35″ × 23″, by P. J. Howard

Photo by P. J. Howard

Photo by Susan Brubaker Knapp

Photo by Linda Stegall

■ P. J.'s sense of humor is evident in her imaginative interpretation of this orchid. The embroidery reads, "Occasionally, just as the fog lifts, you can glimpse *Paphiopedilum lowii* balancing on his viny tightrope. Look quickly. Bright sun frightens him away."

■ Deborah pays homage to pop art and Andy Warhol in this fun piece. She started by manipulating the image in photo-editing software, then printed it on fabric using an inkjet printer, and then added beads.

■ Linda uses three-dimensional elements brilliantly to make this orchid pop off the quilt. Each of the leaves and petals was constructed separately and then appliquéd to the background.

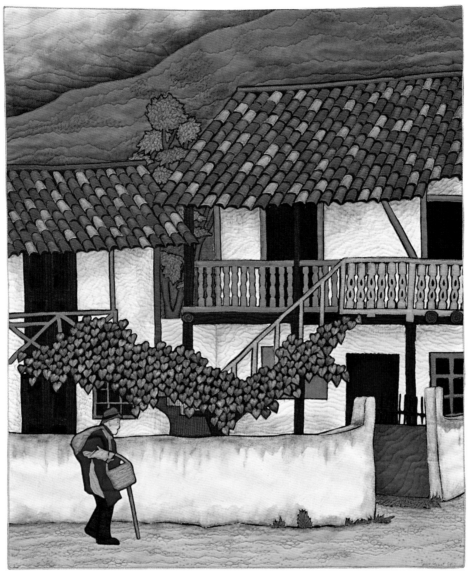

Baños, 26" × 31", by Terry Grant

Photo by Terry Grant

Photo by Ray W. Grant

▨ "I took a lot of liberties with the original photograph," says Terry, "leaving out a lot of details that were distracting and moving things (like the gate) to improve the composition." She also added the figure of a man passing by from a photo taken by her husband.

Sunflower, 36″ × 42″, by Judy Whitehead

■ Judy changed the background and brightened the colors from the original photograph, taken by her friend Jan Dunaway.

Photo by Jan Dunaway

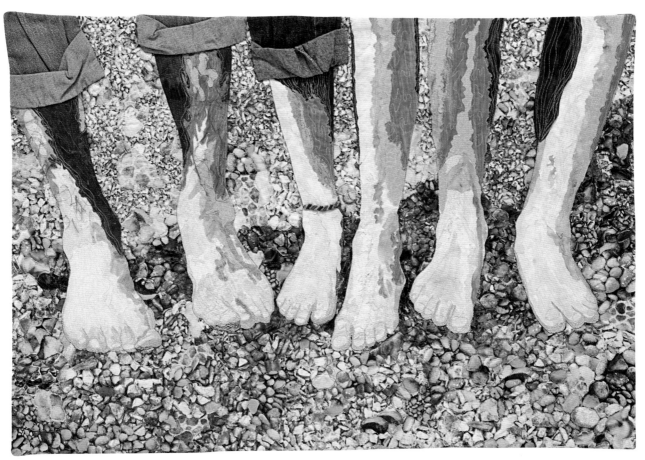

Cold Foot Contest, 32″ × 21¼″, by DeLane Rosenau

Photo by DeLane Rosenau

This was DeLane's very first attempt at translating a photo into a realistic art quilt. It is based on a vacation photo of her husband's and children's feet after a contest to see who could keep their feet in a cold stream the longest.

Blue Buoys, 14″ × 14″, by Sarah Ann Smith

■ While the buoys in Sarah's inspiration photo are bright colors, her piece is a monochromatic color study focusing on value.

Photo by Dwight Pitcairn

Peanut, 17″ × 17″, by Pam George

Pam made this quilt of her daughter's dog, Peanut, as a gift. Her excellent fabric choices and thread sketching make it very lifelike.

Photo by Pam George

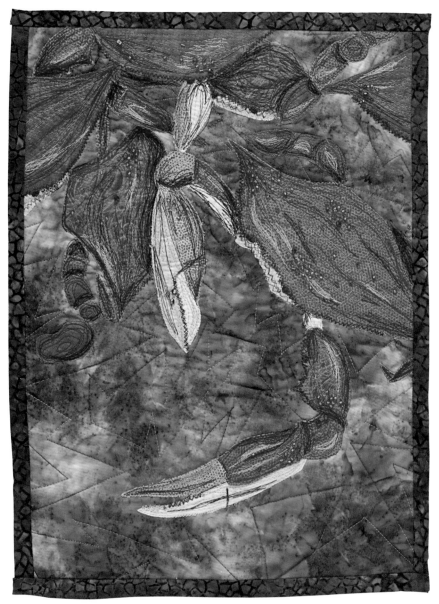

Old Bay, 13½″ × 18½″, by Cary Langhorne Caldwell

■ Cary embellished her quilt with beaded "seasoning" on the cooked crabs.

Photo by Cary Langhorne Caldwell

Ripening, 36″ × 36″, by Nancy G. Cook

Photo by Nancy G. Cook

Nancy starts most of her whole-cloth pieces by taking macro photos or actually scanning her botanical subjects. She then makes a detailed sketch, enlarges it, and makes her pattern from the enlargement. Working on a large piece of hand-dyed fabric, she fills in some areas with Tsukineko inks.

Everglades Strangler, 22½" × 22½", by Greta McCrea

On a hike, Greta asked her husband to take a photo of this tree strangled by another plant so she could interpret it in fabric. Her thread sketching highlights the wonderful textures in the brush and bark.

Photo by Roger S. McCrea

Photo by Patrick Schneider

Susan Brubaker Knapp is a fourth-generation quilter who made her first quilt in 1973 with her mother, a former home economics teacher. It was another twenty years before she made her second quilt, and caught the quilting bug for good. She was soon designing her own quilt patterns.

Having worked in the fields of communications, journalism, and graphic design, Susan was well equipped to begin a pattern business when people started asking about her original designs. Her quilt patterns are now marketed under the name Blue Moon River and carried by several large pattern distributors.

Since 2005, Susan has divided her time between traditional quilts, including lots of needle-turn appliqué, and art quilts. While her core materials—cloth and thread—are the same for both, she often employs nontraditional media, such as fabric paints and dyes, Tyvek, Angelina fibers, and water-soluble wax pastels, to transform the cloth in her fiber art. Her quilts have won national as well as local awards, and have been exhibited at national and international venues.

Susan is the author of *Appliqué Petal Party: A Bouquet of 16 Quilt Blocks and Flowering Border* by C&T Publishing (2009). *Quilting Arts* magazine ran her series of articles on thread sketching throughout 2010 and featured her in segments of *Quilting Arts TV* in 2009 and 2010. Her *Quilting Arts* DVD, *Master Machine Quilting: Free-Motion Stitching and Thread Sketching*, was released in 2009, and a second DVD, *Master Machine Stitching: Thread Sketching Beyond the Basics*, in 2010.

She is an enthusiastic blogger who enjoys connecting with quilters around the world through her blog, which can be accessed through her website, www.bluemoonriver.com. She also does presentations and teaches online, locally, through quilting guilds across the country, and internationally.

Susan is a native of Pittsburgh, Pennsylvania, but now lives near Charlotte, North Carolina, with her husband and daughters.

Also by Susan Brubaker Knapp

Also available as an eBook

Liquitex paints and brushes:

C&T Publishing, Inc.
800-284-1114
www.ctpub.com

Jacquard Lumiere acrylic paint

Dharma Trading
800-542-5227
www.dharmatrading.com

Foils, foil adhesive, and Angelina:

Embellishment Village
877-639-9820
www.embellishmentvillage.com

Foils, foil adhesive, and Angelina:

Interweave Store
800-272-2193
www.interweavestore.com

Foils and Foil Transfer Adhesive:

Laura Murray Designs
612-825-1209
www.lauramurraydesigns.com

Tyvek and foils:

Joggles.com, LLC
401-615-7696
www.joggles.com

Supreme Free-Motion Slider and Sharon Schamber's Quilt Halo:

QuiltPack/LaPierre Studio
239-249-0468
www.freemotionslider.com

Grabaroos gloves:

File Gloves Plus, Inc.
1-877-310-4722
www.grabaroos.com

Great Titles *from* C&T PUBLISHING & STASH BOOKS

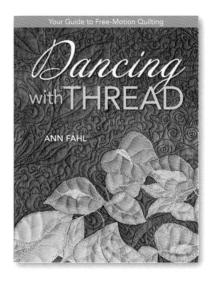

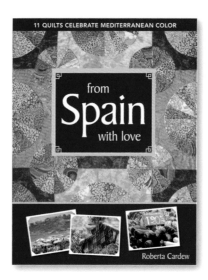

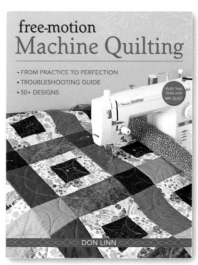

Available at your local retailer or **www.ctpub.com** *or* **800-284-1114**

For a list of other fine books from C&T Publishing, visit our website
to view our catalog online.

C&T PUBLISHING, INC.

P.O. Box 1456
Lafayette, CA 94549
800-284-1114

Email: ctinfo@ctpub.com
Website: www.ctpub.com

C&T Publishing's professional photography services are now available to
the public. Visit us at www.ctmediaservices.com.

Tips and Techniques can be found at www.ctpub.com > Consumer
Resources > Quiltmaking Basics: Tips & Techniques for Quiltmaking & More

For quilting supplies:

COTTON PATCH

1025 Brown Ave.
Lafayette, CA 94549
Store: 925-284-1177
Mail order: 925-283-7883

Email: CottonPa@aol.com
Website: www.quiltusa.com

Note: Fabrics used in the quilts shown may not be currently
available, as fabric manufacturers keep most fabrics in print for
only a short time.